I0069021

ENGINEERING AMERICA

THE RISE OF THE AMERICAN PROFESSIONAL CLASS, 1838-1920

EDITED AND ANNOTATED BY
EDWARD RHODES

WESTPHALIA PRESS
AN IMPRINT OF THE POLICY STUDIES ORGANIZATION

Engineering America:
The Rise of the American Professional Class
1838-1920

All Rights Reserved © 2014 by Policy Studies Organization.
Westphalia Press
An imprint of Policy Studies Organization
1527 New Hampshire Ave., NW
Washington, D.C. 20036
info@ipsonet.org

ISBN-13: 978-1935907862
ISBN-10: 1935907867

Updated material and comments on this edition
can be found at the Westphalia Press website:

www.westphaliapress.org

TABLE OF CONTENTS

ENGINEERING
AMERICA

THE RISE OF THE AMERICAN
PROFESSIONAL CLASS, 1838-1920

Introduction

In a single life-span from 1838 to 1920, America passed through an extraordinary demographic and economic transformation. The raw numbers convey the magnitude of this shift. In that 82-year period, the nation grew from slightly more than 16 million souls to more than 106 million, an increase of greater than six-fold. Gross domestic product increased nearly 22-fold. Per capita income roughly tripled, rising from $1369 to $3848 in 2012 dollars.[1]

Multiple elements combined to yield this explosive growth. Perhaps most obvious was the substantial industrialization of the U.S. economy, based on steel. Steel production, which stood at only 13,000 short tons as late as 1860, exceeded 46 *million* short tons by 1920, an increase of more than 3500-fold.

Associated with industrialization was urbanization. In 1838, only three American cities—the ports of New York, Baltimore, and New Orleans which dominated the export of American agricultural production—had populations in excess of 100,000. Even modest-sized towns were the exception: in all of the United States there were only about 130 places with populations greater than 2500. By 1920, the United States boasted three cities with a population in excess of 1,000,000, and 68 with a population over

1   Historical data are drawn or derived from *Historical Statistics of the United States: Millennial Edition,* http://hsus.cambridge.org/HSUSWeb/HSUSEntryServlet.

100,000. If one describes residents of any place with a population over 2500 as "urban," America's urban population increased from about 1.8 million (roughly 11% of the nation's inhabitants) to nearly 54.3 million (roughly 51%) in this interval. Chicago, which had a population of 4170 in 1838, was a metropolis of 2.7 million in 1920—an increase of nearly 650-fold. Cities such as Detroit and Cleveland experienced growth that, except by comparison with Chicago, was equally astounding—more than 100-fold in Detroit's case and more than 130-fold in Cleveland's.

Making possible this explosive population growth and urbanization was a vast increase in acreage under cultivation. Between 1850 and 1920, acreage devoted to cropland rose from 113 million acres to 347 million, and total acreage in farms (including land for pasture and other agricultural uses) rose from 294 million acres to 879 million—in both cases a rough tripling.

In part this increase in agricultural activity was accomplished by filling up the Upper Midwest (Ohio, Indiana, Illinois, Michigan, and Wisconsin) and the East South-Central states (Kentucky, Tennessee, Alabama, and Mississippi), where substantial acreage was already under cultivation. But in far greater part, it was accomplished by opening up the Great Plains. In 1850, nearly half of America's farmland was to be found in states bordering the Atlantic, and an additional 35% lay east of the Mississippi River. By 1920, the Atlantic seaboard accounted for less than 20% of America's farmland, and well over half lay west of the Mississippi.

This westward expansion of agricultural production was part of a larger geographic shift. In 1838, only two cities north of the Ohio River or west of the Mississippi River had populations greater than 10,000—Cincinnati on the banks of the Ohio and St. Louis at the confluence of the Mississippi and Missouri Rivers. By 1920, the population and economic center of gravity in the United States had moved west. Of course, industrialization and urbanization also hugely impacted the Middle Atlantic states—New York, New Jersey, and Pennsylvania—and to a lesser degree the states of New England and the South Atlantic. But the westward movement of the population, not simply to the industrializing Upper Midwest but to the great agricultural and raw material producing lands of the Great Plains was striking. In 1830, only 3% of the American population lived in the swath of plains from Minnesota and the Dakotas in the north to Louisiana and Texas in the south; by 1890 this had climbed to 12.5%, and by 1920 it was 21.5%.

The creation of an effective, extensive railroad network was a central element in this interconnected process of industrialization, urbanization, agricultural expansion, and geographic shift. Just in the 20 years from 1871 to 1890, the U.S. railroad network expanded from 44,614 miles to 158,037—enough track to go around the earth more than six times, or to go from New York to San Francisco more than 50 times.

The construction of this railroad network was not only critical to the operation of the American economy but also represented a significant element *in* the economy. Railroad construction played an important role in the cyclicality of the American economy in this period. Construction demonstrated a pattern of extraordinary booms and busts: the boom of the early 1870s, with a peak in 1871 when 7,379 miles of new track were laid, was followed by the crash of 1873 and the subsequent long depression, with less than 1,711 miles of new track laid in 1875. The boom of the early 1880s was followed by the downturn of 1883–1885, with the wave peaking at 11,569 miles of new track laid in 1882 and reaching a trough of 2,975 in 1885. While fortunes were made and lost in these cycles, the net effect was an expanding web of economic infrastructure which opened up vast new possibilities for agriculture, raw material extraction, industrial production, and commerce.

To understand this economic expansion it is useful to think about the various factors of production that contributed to it—labor, land, and capital—and about forces influencing the absolute and relative availability of each of these factors over time. Viewed in terms of labor, the period from 1838 to 1920 was one defined by massive immigration, fecundity, and internal migration. Viewed in terms of land, the period was one of easy availability at least until the closing of the frontier in the 1880s, and of relative abundance even thereafter. Annexation of Texas, resolution of the Oregon dispute with Britain, acquisition of California and the southwest following the Mexican War, and—above all—the expansion of the railroad network combined to open up huge territories that could profitably be exploited by American labor.

Obviously, the nearly limitless pool of potentially available labor and the relative abundance of land made the American experience different from that of most other nations during this period. But in many ways it is the story of the third, relatively scare, factor of production—capital—that is perhaps most interesting in gaining an understanding of the emergence of modern America. Capital accumulation posed three separate challenges for the American economy.

First and most obviously, there was the problem of accumulating and concentrating the necessary *financial* capital. In the American system, with government playing a relatively minor part in capital formation, industrialization and the expansion of the railroad network required and enriched private capitalists able to tap into domestic and overseas capital markets. This is the tale of the Carnegies, Morgans, Goulds, and Rockefellers. Whether one chooses to regard these capitalists as villains or heroes, and the rules under which they operated as wicked or wise, private capital formation and government policies that facilitated it were an essential part of how America overcame the potential bottleneck of financial capitalization.

A second potential bottleneck was that of *intellectual* capital. The explosive economic expansion of America in the 1838–1920 period reflected not only the high-octane mix of abundant labor, abundant land, and sufficient financial capital, but the multiplicative impact of a steady stream of new technologies. Reflecting a fortunate intersection of cultural and economic forces and political and legal conditions, this period saw a dynamic outpouring of inventiveness—both domestic and "borrowed," the latter reflecting an ability to gain access to (as well as to improve upon) European inventions and to attract inventors from

Europe.[2] The number of patents issued annually rose from about 500 in 1838 to more than 37,000 in 1920, and in many ways this statistic measures simply the tip of the huge, submerged iceberg of creativity. (The total number of patent *applications* in the single year of 1920 was just shy of 92,000: the difference between applications and grants presumably gives some sense of how many creative minds were working on the same problems, and in some cases coming up with similar solutions.)

It is the third element of capital accumulation, however, that this present study focuses on: the problem of *human* capital. The explosive growth of the American economy and equally jaw-dropping transformation of American society in the 1838–1920 period demanded not only the availability of labor, land, financial capital, and new technology but a dramatic expansion in the nation's collective human ability to use these.

Where did this human capital come from? How did an agrarian society, operating under largely decentralized, weak governance, manage to produce the vastly increased number of, and vastly more skilled, professionals that it needed? Money does not keep equipment in working order, nor do new inventions build and operate themselves. The economic expansion of the nation and the emergence of modern America required the rise of an American professional class.

---

2   As in later periods, American scientific and technological progress benefited enormously from the openness of America and its ability to tap into intellectual and human capital produced elsewhere. American steel production, for example, was jump-started by access to the British-developed Bessemer process, which then was improved by American Alexander Lyman Holley (1832–1882); in the electric communication field, America profited from the fact that Alexander Graham Bell's ongoing work took place in the United States and Canada.

Oₙₑ — **O**ne approach to understanding the rise of the American professional class—doctors, lawyers, scientists, managers, and, above all, engineers—is through macro-level study of this class as a whole. Such an approach focuses, for example, on aggregate data regarding numbers of individuals in particular professions, their income, the "production" of college graduates, and laws and regulations affecting professional certification. A second, also useful approach, however, is the micro one, looking at particular life stories. This approach requires that we give the same sort of careful attention to the life history of professionals as has been given to documenting and analyzing the life history of particular financial capitalists and particular inventors.

There are obvious dangers to any micro approach, and one should be careful to avoid generalizations based on close observation of a few individuals. Each life is idiosyncratic.

Nonetheless, close examination of an individual life can be revealing, permitting the observer to explore the actual dynamics at work—to see how particular cultural influences, particular economic realities, and particular social pressures combined in particular historical conditions to yield particular decisions, particular patterns of action, and particular outcomes. Understanding how, at a micro level, these forces actually interact can provide critical insight into the organic processes through which human capital is produced. This makes possible not only richer, more realistic modeling at the macro level but serves to warn against simplistic, "one-size-fits-all" prescriptions for generating human capital or promoting social and economic change.

This volume offers a case study examination of one professional—a civil engineer responsible for building and then operating substantial stretches of the Santa Fe railroad system that economically opened up large parts of Kansas, Colorado, Oklahoma, and north Texas—and his pathway from in an impoverished, rural, *petit-bourgeois* background. It is precisely the ordinariness of this history that makes it valuable, and helps us to understand how America overcame its shortfall in human capital and the cultural, social, economic, and political factors shaping this process.

In addition to the problem of generalizability that bedevils any micro-level study, there is a second problem to be acknowledged regarding the epistemological and methodological approach adopted in this volume. This volume is not simply biographical, it is autobiographical. The observer in our case is the subject himself. The usual interplay between the historian and his material is complicated by the fact that the historian *is* his material.

Obviously, any autobiographical account is only indirectly an account of what happened or why it happened. More directly it is an account of what, deliberately or accidentally, the subject reveals about what he or she believes happened and why. Every sentence in an autobiography needs to be prefaced with the statement: "This is what I choose to tell you about what I think occurred and about what I think were the factors that led to this occurrence."

It is, however, precisely this insight into what a participant believes is worth recording and proper to record (and what, by exclusion, the participant believes is *not* worth recording or proper to record) and into the causality and relationships that the participant claims were at work that makes an autobiography valuable to the social scientist.

Several factors—beyond the fact that it exists at all—arguably make this particular autobiography unusual. The first is its surprising factual accuracy and detail. While the author sometimes misspells the names of individuals with whom he interacted and makes minor errors in the dates of certain childhood events, the events, occurrences, places, and activities he describes are nearly perfectly consistent with historical records and with other available documents. The *facts* are right. The reader is therefore able to focus on which facts have been included, which have been excluded, and what meaning has been proposed for these facts.

The second is the level of candor. This presumably reflects the fact that this manuscript was never intended for public reading, much less publication. The internal and external evidence suggests that it was intended for private reading by an audience of three: the author's two nephews and his niece.

The third is the degree of introspection. This presumably is a consequence of the pedagogical intent of the manuscript—it was intended to allow the next generation to draw lessons from the author's life. In its musings and tone, however, there is also a suggestion that the author self-consciously used the exercise of composing this document as a means of trying to gain greater clarity in his own mind as to the meaning and purpose of his life. The author of this manuscript was wrestling with many of the same questions that we, the current readers, are wrestling with. How did he get from his childhood roots to his professional career, and what were the forces and influences that made this happen?

❧

The author and subject of this study, Daniel Harker Rhodes, was a contemporary of the great financial capitalists of the Gilded Age.[3] The internal and external evidence suggests that Rhodes wrote and revised the memoir over an 11-year period, from 1900 to 1911.

Rhodes was born out-of-wedlock in rural New Jersey in 1838. Apart from his illegitimacy, there was nothing particularly unusual in his family background. His mother's family——the Predmores and Harkers—were early New Jersey settlers. The Predmores were among the first residents of what is now New Brunswick, New Jersey (earlier known as "Pridmore's Swamp") in the 1680s, moving after several generations to Sussex County in the far northwestern corner of the state. The Harkers arrived in Massachusetts Bay a few years after the Mayflower and, moving with the forward edge of settlement, were associated with the early English settlements in Rhode Island, Long Island, and coastal New Jersey, before

---

3   Andrew Carnegie was born in 1835, three years before Rhodes; Jay Gould, in 1836; J.P. Morgan, in 1837; and John D. Rockefeller Jr., in 1839.

eventually moving to what was then the new frontier in Sussex County. The family of the author's adoptive father, John Rhodes, arrived in New Jersey in 1745 when John Rhodes's grandfather, a 20-year-old midshipman in the Royal Navy, "jumped ship," set himself up as a merchant and schoolmaster, married the daughter of a prosperous Dutch farmer, and, in the 1760s, moved to the Sussex frontier as an early settler, miller, and landowner in what became Stillwater Township. The Predmores, Harkers, Rhodeses, and their collateral kin were prolific, and were generally comfortably situated by the modest standards of the rural society. Some were farmers; many were occupied in rural trades and occupations—millers, school teachers, keepers of public houses, village merchants. They frequently held positions of public trust, such as justice of the peace or county clerk.

Daniel Harker was his mother's eldest child, born when she was still single but already past a typical marrying age. The author's adoptive father, John Rhodes, had already raised a brood of children; a widower, his marriage to Daniel Harker's mother came late in his mid-life. Past the peak of their personal and economic health, together they had four additional children. The economy of northwestern New Jersey was in transition. By the time of Daniel Harker's birth, families were already leaving Sussex County for points further west, to acquire better or larger farms in upstate New York or Ohio. The remaining farms were modestly modernizing and capitalizing to take advantage of improved transportation and to meet the needs of the growing markets of Philadelphia and New York. The Rhodes family's repeated moves around northwestern New Jersey in search of better economic prospects, and ultimate relocation to the Finger Lakes region of New York State, were not atypical.

Rhodes received a typical primary school education of the day. As an adolescent he sampled various possible careers—milling, dairy farming, mill construction, farming—before learning the tinsmithing and hardware trade. At age 23, on the cusp of setting up on his own, he enlisted with most of the young men in his community for nine months service in the Civil War. He completed his military service unharmed except for a bout with the mumps which may well have left him sterile. The war experience also exposed him to economic and commercial conditions outside the New Jersey–Pennsylvania–New York region and to the railroad- and steamship-based technological revolution underway. It seems, too, to have encouraged him to consider wider personal and professional horizons. Rather than opening up shop as a tinsmith, after mustering out Rhodes pursued a high school and then college education. Lacking the financial resources for such study, Rhodes was the beneficiary of local philanthropy: a highly successful financial capitalist invested in Rhodes, advancing him, at interest, the money needed.

Graduating from the University of Michigan as a civil engineer in 1869, Rhodes entered into the boom-and-bust cyclical economy of railroad construction and operation, first in the Upper Midwest—Michigan, Ohio, and Indiana—and then, when the long depression of 1873–1879 finally ended, very successfully with the Atchison, Topeka, and Santa Fe Railroad in Kansas,

Colorado, and Oklahoma. At the end of his career, he turned from railroading to mining, operating and providing seed-capital for a number of zinc- and lead-mines in southwestern Missouri.

Though Rhodes does not appear to have viewed it so, this professional life was hard in a number of dimensions, most obviously the personal ones. Rhodes did not marry until he was 50; lived in boarding houses or hotels until he was in his mid-50s; and did not live long enough in any one place to put down any significant roots until he was in his 60s.

For a modern reader interested in understanding the rise of the American professional class and the emergence of a recognizably modern America, Rhodes's analysis of his life offers a number of interesting insights—many of them by omission.

1. Calvinism. Perhaps the single most obvious theme—sometimes explicit, but nearly always a sub-text—in Rhodes's account is the pervasive impact of Calvinist thought. Though there is little indication that Rhodes was necessarily a very active churchgoer, and he never formally became a church member, Rhodes's account begins with his mother's Presbyterianism, and he never strays far from these roots. The references to Presbyterianism do not appear to be idle ones, but rather reflect an essential element in Rhodes's understanding of himself and his purpose. Both in terms of teachings about daily life and in terms of deeper assumptions about human nature and human calling, Rhodes appears to have absorbed Calvinism deeply and fully. The evidence seems consistent with Rhodes's self-appraisal that he despised idleness, viewed alcohol and life's other distractions warily, and rigidly stayed away from gambling (except "investment" gambling, in concerns such as lead- and zinc-mines—and even this he seems to regard as something of a weakness). Rhodes's work ethic was impressive.

More profoundly, though, Rhodes seems to have possessed substantial confidence in divine grace— that God possessed a plan for him and was steering his course. Reason, knowledge, and technology were tools given by God with the expectation that they would be used fully to meet the challenges and opportunities presented by God's grace. In this understanding, it is easy to see how Rhodes saw his work as a "calling." Though from Rhodes's personal correspondence it is clear that he was not entirely the cold, detached individual that comes across in his memoir—his own letters reveal close personal attachments, a clear and compassionate understanding of the complicated psychology of his correspondents, and a playful wit, and the letters sent to him indicate the closeness that his correspondents felt to him—it seems equally clear that Rhodes understood his personal relationships as fundamentally built upon the duties and obligation that, thanks to God's grace, he owed these others.

2. *Family.* Family plays a complex and complicated role in Rhodes's account, often represented as something of a grail—an idealized goal to be pursued, but absent in present existence. What is perhaps most interesting, however, is the unremarked-upon but striking evolution of the nature of actual "family" during Rhodes's life. Family in his childhood and young adulthood was a widely-extended community, including vast numbers of cousins, uncles, and aunts, between whose homes individuals moved fairly easily for shorter or longer stays and upon whom

they relied for social insurance—e.g., to be nursed in infirmity or in final days. Travel, discovery of new economic possibilities, and, ultimately, economic livelihood depended on this family network. By the mid-1860s, however, Rhodes had abandoned this extended family (though it continued to function for those relatives that remained in more traditional lifestyles). Family and its reciprocal obligations continued to exist but were defined far more narrowly: for Rhodes, the family circle narrowed to two of his brothers and their families, for whom he accepted responsibility.

In place of extended family, Rhodes turned to non-familial social and professional networks. Beginning with his return from the Civil War, Rhodes turned to individuals outside the family network for assistance, first in gaining an education and then in gaining employment. Particularly important was the network of University of Michigan classmates. Not only did this initially launch him with survey work in the Great Lakes and with Midwestern railroads, it was this network that brought him to the Santa Fe road and that assisted him in moving forward quickly there. While informal networks were of special importance, Rhodes was also aware of the value of more formal social networks, in his case the Masons and the Grand Army of the Republic.

3. Education. Education was a key enabler for Rhodes, making possible the jump from a career as a local merchant and tinsmith to the world of a successful professional. The possibility of this education was based on several elements. First, generally available primary education provided foundational literacy and mathematical skills sufficient for craft and white-collar employment and a value system consistent with seeking further education. Second, secondary-level academies were widespread; enrollment in these was not restricted by class or family background, and financial hurdles while significant were not insurmountable. Third, colleges were widely available and provided practical professional education; as with secondary education, enrollment was not restricted by class or family background, and young scholars often found it possible to work their way through school, by taking time off to teach or to work in other positions. In Rhodes's narrative, education played two of the key roles that it is typically credited with playing in American society today—providing needed intellectual capital and professional networks. Interestingly, there is no indication in Rhodes's story that it played the third role that it is now commonly described as playing—certifying an individual as qualified.

Arguably, the Civil War also played an important educational role for Rhodes. Certainly, the disruptive impact of the Civil War in his life is worth special note. It broke the natural flow of Rhodes's life, as it must have done for many other young men. And it provided a dramatic expansion of the world with which Rhodes was familiar. For the first time he saw, at least in passing, significant urban centers—Newark, Philadelphia, Baltimore, Washington, Cincinnati. While he was already familiar with railroads and with riverboats, the war showed him the enormous impact that transportation networks could play in moving people and products quickly. And the war also exposed him to a range of local economic conditions and modes of production.

4. *Private philanthropy.* Both directly and indirectly, Rhodes's path into the professional class was made

possible, or at least made much easier, by private philanthropy. Whether Rhodes would ultimately have found it possible to go to college without private loans is unclear, but certainly his progress was speeded by private support. Indirectly, too, the pathway was facilitated by private philanthropy: the academy at which he prepped was the recipient of private patronage. Whether the academy could have operated without this patronage is again unclear— but certainly the ability of the academy's principal to allow Rhodes to attend without paying tuition must have been made easier by the academy's solid financial base. This private philanthropy came neither through church or state channels. It was, in Rhodes's understanding, a generous response to Rhodes's demonstrated merit, provided by individuals who had the opportunity to observe and judge what he might be able to contribute to the world.

5. *Class and social mobility.* The absence of class or social barriers to entry into the professional class is both a striking and a critical element in Rhodes's story. Examination of the life histories of Rhodes's professional colleagues suggests that Rhodes's experience is typical in this regard: his professional colleagues were the children of rural craftsmen, school teachers, modest farmers, and the like. Equally interesting, however, is the essentially complete absence of any reference to class or social status in Rhodes's memoir. Indeed, the only place in the memoir where Rhodes refers to class, social standing, or family background is in the preface, where he is at pains to make it clear that his biological father was not some itinerant farm laborer. But this passage is striking by its uniqueness. Class does not figure in Rhodes's account. In his daily professional life, we know that Rhodes interacted

with the full spectrum of American society, from wealthy East Coast financiers to immigrant laborers, indigent camp-followers, and urban and rural poor. In his discussion of his professional life there is no reference to this. In those private notes in which he discusses some of his interactions with itinerant cowboys, the principal theme is one of their camaraderie, generosity, and shared humanity—even while noting the roughness of their entertainment and tendency toward excessive use firearms in that entertainment.

6. Physical mobility. One of the ubiquitous features of Rhodes's life and narrative was physical mobility. His entry into the professional class and pursuit of a professional career was predicated on his ability to move immediately and rapidly around the country. This extraordinary physical mobility in turn depended not simply on his willingness to move at a moment's notice but on the social and physical infrastructure that allowed it. Obviously, a communication and transportation infrastructure—that is, a telegraph and railroad network—that permitted an employer in one city to reach Rhodes in another city, and for him in a matter of a few days to take up new employment, was essential. Less obvious, perhaps, was the financial network that permitted individuals and employers to move payment and wealth easily. Even less obvious because of its pervasiveness was the physical and social infrastructure that allowed individuals to find housing, board, and the other necessities of life in a new location on a moment's notice—and to abandon old residences equally quickly. As a "stranger," Rhodes could and did arrive in town, set up shop, employ assistance, and start work, literally overnight and without difficulty.

7. Race, ethnicity, and gender. Given the times in which Rhodes lived, it is remarkable that neither race nor ethnicity play a part in his account. There is an indication that he meant to talk about native Americans in his discussion of railroading in what was then the Indian Territory and is now Oklahoma. But there is nowhere a mention of slavery or of Black Americans—indeed these are absent even from his contemporaneous Civil War notes. Similarly, there is no mention or discussion of immigration or the substantial ethnic shift that took place in the United States in the post-Civil War period. As with social class, race and ethnicity are striking by their absence.

Gender, too, is remarkable for its absence. While the two women who figure in any significant way in Rhodes's narrative—his mother and his first wife—both occupied traditional home-making roles, neither was dependent on men. As Rhodes makes a point of noting, his mother maintained a separate household before her marriage, and his wife moved west as a single, widowed woman. The other women in Rhodes's smaller, more nuclear family seem to have been regarded by him in terms largely undifferentiated from their husbands or brothers. Private correspondence makes absolutely clear that Rhodes saw nothing unusual or bothersome about the fact that in later life one of his sisters-in-law became a very successful hotel operator and owner, supporting and doting upon her invalided husband. In his personal writing, Rhodes's correspondents appear to have been as likely to be women as men, and there are very few passages in Rhodes's various writings that are discordant with current sensibilities.

8. Politics. Again, this is remarkable by its absence. In private notes, Rhodes acknowledges that although he was raised in a Democrat household, his first presidential vote was for Abraham Lincoln; from other sources we know that as an adult Rhodes was identified as a Republican. But this is virtually all we have recorded regarding his political views. Nowhere in his writing does one find comment on the momentous political contests of the day, or of the underlying issues, such as the tariff, or free silver, or trust-busting, or the Spanish-American War, or imperialism.

9. Technology. Like Calvinism, technology is a theme that runs the length of Rhodes's memoir, starting with loving descriptions of how folding desks operated in his earliest one-room schoolhouse. Rhodes's disinterest in his political world was fully matched by his interest in his physical world and in how this could be transformed.

❧

What emerges from Rhodes's self-portrait is thus in many ways a striking model of the "modern," liberal American. Rhodes's account of himself is of an individual deeply imbued with a Calvinist ethic but not formally religious or divisively sectarian; attached to a nuclear family and viewing family as the essential social building block, but relying on wider social and professional networks; committed to education both as a pathway to economic self-improvement and as desirable in itself; free from any sense of debt to or reliance on the state or the church; unmarked by any strong class identification and seeing no class-based barriers to mobility; tied to no fixed geographic location and willing and expecting to move frequently; largely blind to questions of race and ethnicity and comfortable with "strong," independent women; uninterested in politics and fascinated by technology.

Perhaps one of the clearest indications of Rhodes's "modernity" is his puzzlement about the measures against which he should judge his life. Despite his Calvinist certainties—and his belief in progress and reason and order and action—in writing his memoirs, Rhodes yields to doubts about the meaning of his own life and about the measures against which it should be judged. Arguably, in this, too, one may find a metaphor for the emergence of modernity and the rise of the American professional class.

Autobiography

of

Daniel Harker Rhodes

Above: Daniel Harker Rhodes.

In the neighborhood of the Predmore home at New Patterson, N.J., there lived a family named Pittinger. Owned their farm. Were of good repute. Prominent in church and society. The same social status as the Predmore families. Pittinger had a son about the age of Miss Margaret Ann Predmore. The two had grown from childhood to young manhood and womanhood near each other. They became lovers and he asked Miss M.A. Predmore to be his wife. As it promised happiness, he was accepted, time was set for the marriage ceremony. He was false to his engagement. The marriage was never consummated. From the confidences and intimacy of the engagement year a son was born to the Pittinger boy and Miss M.A. Predmore. His name is of recorded [sic] in the family bible as Daniel Harker Pittinger. This boy was between five and six years old when Miss Predmore married John Rhodes. After this marriage the boy, D.H. Pittinger took the name of Rhodes and was known as D.H. Rhodes the rest of his life time. The circumstances connected with the parentage of the child were well known by everyone and Miss Predmore was thought none the less of. She was, and continued to her death, a member of the Presbyterian Church, a devotedly Christian woman.

After Mother's death the above was told me by one who was familiar with the circumstances. Also, that from her childhood Mother had been an active member of the Presbyterian Church. I have traits of character inherited from him by which I know him to have been a high bred man, notwithstanding his being false to his engagement, and his betrayal of a too confiding young woman.[4]

❦

---

4   Preface to Rhodes's autobiography, written in his hand on the cover in ink, with erasures and corrections. The remainder of the autobiography, in the same notebook, is a clean copy in his hand in pencil, clearly transcribed from other notes. From the references—e.g., to the family bible—the source of Rhodes's information was presumably his maternal uncle and namesake, Daniel Harker Predmore. The family name was Pittenger, not "Pittinger" as Rhodes renders it. There is no indication in any preserved documents that Rhodes ever knew or sought out a relationship with any of his biological father's family or that he even knew the given name of his biological father. Perhaps contrary to the impression Rhodes gives of a young girl in the first blush of womanhood, Margaret Ann Predmore was 28 years old at the time Rhodes was born. Interestingly, this is the only place in the autobiography in which Rhodes makes reference to social "status" or class, or to genetic inheritance. One possible explanation for the inclusion of these references here, and for the addition of this preface, is that the fact of Rhodes's illegitimacy may not have been known to the nephew to whom the autobiography was entrusted.

I was born December 24th/25th, 1838, near New Patterson, Sussex County, New Jersey and spent my early childhood there. My Mother's maiden name was Margaret Ann Predmore, sister of John Predmore and Daniel Predmore of Sussex County. My Grandfather Predmore I remember nothing of, but do remember Grandmother Predmore as a very old lady occupying her high back chair at the corner of the old fireplace. Walked unsteadily with a cane. One morning when I was about three or four years old, there was an unusual stir in the house. Grandmother was found dead in her bed, lying on her back and I remember hearing them say there was no signs of any struggle whatever, she had died quietly and peacefully of old age.[5]

---

5   A village in Stillwater Township, New Jersey, New Patterson is now known as Swartswood. About six miles west of Newton, the county seat of Sussex County, Swartswood was then and still is a rural crossroads in the foothills of the Kittatinny Mountains of far northwestern New Jersey. Margaret Ann Predmore (1810–1858), Rhodes's mother, was by nearly six years the youngest of her parents' 10 children—presumably a surprise in her parents' "old age." Daniel Harker Predmore (1789–1867), Rhodes's namesake, was Margaret Ann Predmore's oldest brother. Nearly 21 years her senior (and with a daughter only two years younger than she), Daniel Harker Predmore appears to have played something of a parental role, and was the head of the Predmore clan while Rhodes was growing up. Rhodes's maternal grandfather, Joseph Predmore (1767–1839), died at age 72 when Rhodes was three months old. Rhodes was actually five-and-a-half when his maternal grandmother, Margaret Harker Predmore (1769–1844), passed away, just shy of her 75th birthday.

My first school days were spent in the old frame school house that stood in the parting of the roads—one running through the village, the other leaving it to the left and going up what was then called Decker Mountain or Sprout Hill. The house was used also for religious services and here with my Mother, I first remember attending church. The preacher was a Reverend T.B. Conditt, who also preached at Swartswood and, I think, Newton. My first teacher was a Mr. Packard, relative of the Rev. Mr. Conditt.[6]

---

6   The building that Rhodes refers to was erected in 1833, at the head of what is now called Sprout Hill Road, just north of Swartswood and some 2.5 miles northwest of the still-extant 1855 Stillwater church building.

The Reverend T.B. (Thaniel Beers) Condit (1804–1888) was pastor of the First Presbyterian Church of Stillwater from 1837 to 1881, and in that role also served the Swartswood Presbyterian Church. Though called to a different career and a generation older, in terms of social mobility T.B. Condit provides an interesting parallel to Rhodes. The oldest son in a family of 10, Condit learned the shoemaking trade in rural New Jersey, just across the Morris County line from Sussex County. Believing himself called to the ministry, he pursued a course of self-education, and was ordained in 1837. Despite the humble background and rural setting, Condit's household in Stillwater seems to have been an educated and globally aware one, and Condit seems to have been a path-breaker for his younger siblings. Condit himself authored two books—*Morning, Noon and Night, or Christ in Every Page* and *The Bible Reader's Guide,* published in 1863. Two of his sisters—Azubah (1806–1844) and Maria (1808–1886)— went to India on Presbyterian missionary work, Azubah marrying there; one of his brothers —Isaiah (1817–1911)— became a doctor and another—Hiram (1821–1902)— became a successful lawyer. The upward mobility of the next generation is even more marked: Condit's older son, Elbert Nevius (1846–1900), was educated at Princeton, ordained, and served as president of Occidental College and of the Albany Collegiate Institute (the forerunner to Lewis and Clark College); Condit's other son, Isaac Hiram (1848–1930), was also educated at Princeton, ordained, and taught mathematics and classics at Albany Institute before returning to New Jersey and serving as pastor at another Presbyterian Church in Stillwater Township; and Condit's three daughters all were educated — one at the Boston Conservatory of Music—and taught at private schools, at Albany Institute, and, in one case, in northern India. George Washington Packard (1810–1877), Rhodes's first teacher, was married to T.B. Condit's sister Tryphena (1813–1896).

The old schoolhouse was a characteristic one for those days. There were only rude benches in the body of the house, no desks. On both sides of the room were leaves hinged against the joists. In front of these were plank seats supported by legs of round sticks driven in holes bored through the plank—two legs at each end of each seat. Each hinged leaf was, as I remember, about five or six feet long and the seats of corresponding lengths. The seats had no backs, simply rude benches. The leaves and benches occupied the whole of the two sides of the schoolroom. When not in use the leaves would be dropped down, like those of a table and Sundays the seats would be pushed back against them. This gave more room for the chairs or stools that people would bring with them to sit in. When seated at the desks the pupils faced the side of the room, backs to the interior of the room. The side seats were so high I could not begin to reach the floor with my feet, but the benches in the middle of the room were low and for such I was then.

The only grades in the school, as I remember, was when one's legs got long enough to reach the floor on the side benches, he was moved from the low seats to the side, and that was an event in the pupils' school life. I never reached a grade in that school.

The mode of punishment was the switch and leather strap. There was nothing unwarranted about either—strictly business. The boys mostly had to cut their own switches. Small as I was before I left that school, I well remember having to go out and cut a switch to be whipped with. Fortunately, or otherwise, brush came close to the schoolhouse and a thick growth of swamp whortleberry bushes[7] three or four hundred feet from the schoolhouse furnished, it seemed to me, a never-failing source of supply. Oh, that berry patch brings painful recollections for the whips it furnished, and pleasant memories of the delicious berries it furnished us school children in their season. (Sometimes we ate the berries while green—couldn't wait for them to ripen!) How true it is that from our earliest childhood to latest life, ever the bitter with the sweet; pain is ever the shadow to pleasure.

At one end of this school room was the only door and beside it on the rude bench stood the water blickey [ed.: tin pail]. At the opposite end was the seat of government. The incentive to learning was growing out in the bush or lay secure with the archives of the government. I doubt if ever Emperor ruled with more despotic sway a more unruly set, but from the distance "dim and long" come recollections of his sacrifices and kindly interests as well and we cherish his memory as we do the memory of the dear old songs that lulled us to rest in infancy.

The wood for our schoolhouse fire, mostly donated by patrons of the school, was cut green, being hauled in big sled loads, logs and limbs twelve or fourteen feet long, and dumped off for the teacher (generally the teacher) or the larger boys to chop up—or freeze. It fell to the lot of us younger ones to go out and strip the bark off the fence rails and dead trees for kindling. With our little load, we often returned crying and almost frozen. No provision was made for drones in that hive.

---

7   Presumably V*accinium corymbosum,* sometimes also known as the bilberry, a cousin of the European blueberry.

The old home—still there in 1900 as I write these lines—stood on the left side of the road going from [New] Patterson to Newton and perhaps forty rods from the [New] Patterson to Swartswood road. It was a story and a half house. A stoned up well with curb, high corner posts, windlass, and oaken bucket was but a few feet from the front door. There was a plot of ground about two hundred feet square, as I remember, with the house. My Mother bought this place herself before she was married and she and her Mother lived there when she was married. On one side of the living room was a large open fireplace with its crane, hooks and trammels, shovel and tongs. An immense pair of andirons with fancy ball top knobs was ample to hold the smaller wood as frontispiece to the great back log. The wood was usually provided in winter by making a frolic, when all the friends would come for an afternoon and haul logs and limbs, length of the sled, that had been cut usually beforehand in some friendly wood. In the evening a supper and usually a dance. No charge was made, but one went to the other's frolic. This wood was usually cut as wanted. The fireplace took four foot wood and there was little need for kindling in winter, at least, for the fire seldom went out on the hearth entirely.[8]

---

8   Ever with an eye to how life's practical problems were to be solved, in his notes for the manuscript, Rhodes provides a lengthier description of the problem of maintaining a flame in the household:

> "When, on account of absence from home for a few days or other cause, it did [go out], some one went to a neighbor and got a few coals of fire. A favorite way of carrying them was between two pieces of bark, these curled sufficiently to hold the coals. I do not remember that there were matches at this date, but the flint and box of punk were used to start a fire. That way was easiest.

I knew of no such furniture as a stove those days. The baking was done in an outside brick oven—built in one side of the fireplace, or outside the house—or in a tin bake oven before the fireplace, as was most convenient.[9] In a corner of the room near the fireplace stood a high cupboard with drawers and doors used for table linen, dishes, and a world of things of interest to a small boy. The upper part was entirely out of my reach even on a chair as I found often by experience. It was a mine that I could explore only at general house cleaning. How I did revel in its mysteries at such times and hunt for knives and toys Mother had hidden from [me]. The top part of this cupboard was also a favorite and only really convenient place, *it seemed*, for the tin pan of crullers [ed: twisted, fried pastries]. I could see the dish and scent the cakes, "only that and nothing more." Tantalus to his chin in water, dying of thirst is a fitting symbol of the small boy under such circumstances.

Phosphorous matches were introduced commercially in Europe in 1833. Their great convenience soon brought them into use in cities and towns. Probably were used to some extent in this country at the time I am writing of, but I do not remember having seen any till later. Another way of insuring against loss of fire was by filling a vessel, usually a saucer, with grease. In this was put some candle wicking or as often, a strip of muslin, one end of which lay over the edge of the dish above the oil. If the strip was small, this would burn for a day or more according to the amount of grease in the dish."

9   Again, Rhodes's notes contain a longer explanation of the practical issues of the time and the technology for their solution:

"As it took some time to heat up the brick oven, for quick work there was a tin bake oven made to set on the hearth in front of the fireplace fire. It was open toward the fire, and the cover was sloping like a shed roof. This both confined the heat and reflected it upon the pan holding the dough. Meat could also be baked in it. This oven was in almost daily use, as the brick oven was only fired once or twice a week in small households."

In the bedroom where Grandmother died was Mother's trunk—a wood body covered with calfskin, tanned with the hair on. The calf's hair, like Joseph's coat was of many colors—white, brown, and black in spots, all of which gave the trunk a variegated appearance. The covering was fastened on with large oval-head brass tacks, giving it a substantial and aristocratic air. On the oval top, in large letters formed with the same brass tacks were the letters, M.A.P., Mother's initials. To save me painful experiences, it was always locked, and when it was opened to get some extra nice piece of apparel, the perfume from the trunk was like that from "Araby the blest" so fragrant was it, and if by stealth I got an opportunity to tumble things about and rummage it just a little, I would find scattered through it rose leaves—sacks of fragrant powders and herbs, but my time was always too *limited* to explore all its mysteries, so that trunk was ever a mystery still.

On the walls of the rooms hung pictures common in those days. One was "Elizabeth and Her Pet" — lady and her dog with blond and curly hair. Another, "The Young Mother" —Mother and babe. Another, "The Empress" —of any country you liked, and so on. All the figures were as stiff in pose and unnatural as if cut from pasteboard. The poorest lithograph on the poorest brand of tobacco is high art compared with the best prints of that time.

My bed was just at the top of the stairs, head against the chimney. Mother would usually take me up to bed, hear me repeat that prayer so dear to a Mother's heart when said by her younger children, "Now I lay me down to sleep," tuck me in, give me the seal of her love, and leave me for the night. If it did not rain, all usually went well until morning. But if it rained, the noise on the roof would waken me and if hard, I would become terrified and scream until they took me down stairs. In this chamber stood the great spinning wheel, the flax wheel, and the yarn reel. Mother would card the wool, make the rolls and spin all the yarn needed for the family hose and mittens. It seems to me now, what boyish pleasure to be up there with her when spinning—that to and fro in harmony with the humming of the spindle, the reverse to wind the thread, the halt to join another roll, then the whirl of the wheel and the humming again. How vividly it all comes back to one at times! My part was, principally, to get in the way, hold a stick against the wheel spokes to hear it clatter, or whirl the yarn reel to hear it swap revolutions, until I would be ordered down stairs "immediately," to play out of doors, "like a good boy." Often, however, it was cold, or stormed, then I had my innings. But I know we both enjoyed those many hours, for Mother was nearly always singing in a tone that seemed to be in harmony with the hum of the busy wheel.

During all these early days Father was so busily engaged at milling during the day and evening that, at this distance, it seems that Mother was my home companion.

In a corner of the home place, diagonally from the house stood the barn, and a lane led to the highway. At the proper season the garden was a veritable flowerbed, as it seems to me now. As I

remember, almost every variety of flowering peren-
nials, fancy grasses, and fragrant herbs were there.
The garden was always Mother's delight, and my
Nemesis, for it required water; and when it came to
wetting the garden, washing feet, face, and hands,
water and I were always out. The flower garden flou-
rished; it was, in part, watered with tears.

At the time this refers to, New Patterson had a
small tavern, kept by George W. Dodder, a cousin of
ours,[10] one store, shoe and blacksmith shop, saw mill,
tannery, schoolhouse, and a few straggling dwellings.
At this time (1900) it is a summer resort for city people
with ample hotel accommodations. Swartswood lake,
a beautiful sheet of water half a mile away affords fine
boating and fishing.

Letters were not put in envelopes. The two sides
of the paper were folded in, the ends brought together
and one end slipped inside the other, and a wafer seal
slipped between the folds and sealed. As the sheet was
usually much longer than wide, this was easily done.
It cost ten cents postage to send the letter by mail.
Our first move from the early home to which we never
as a family returned occurred one April day when I
was about ten years old. We went to live near Uncle
William Rhodes' in North Vernon, Sussex County.
Father's brother. I spurned to ride with the wagons and

---

10   Not unusually for this time in rural New Jersey, where families were
often large but the number of families (and eligible partners) small, George
Wintermute Dodder (1815–1898) was related to Rhodes in several ways.
Dodder himself was a first cousin of Rhodes's adopted father; Dodder's wife,
Effie Jane Predmore (1821–1893), was the daughter of Rhodes's namesake
uncle, Daniel Harker Predmore.

walked all the way with Father, helping him with the stock. I will never forget the trials of that day. It was too far for me, but we got through by evening.[11] Father ran a sawmill for Uncle William; also, in the season, a water power cider mill. We lived in a house near the mill. House is now torn away, no trace of it left. I attended school at the old North Vernon Schoolhouse, probably still standing. Among my schoolmates were John and Susan Carpenter, Alfred and Julia Toland, Charles and George Crissey, Charles Baxter and sister Kate. Daniel Bailey was a Captain in Army in the Civil War.[12] Sister Lydia Ann was born at New Patterson and

---

11   North Vernon is now known as Glenwood, a village in Vernon Township, New Jersey, a stone's throw from the New York State line. Twenty-four miles northeast of Swartswood, Glenwood would indeed have been a long day's trek for a boy. It was, however, a familiar one for families in both neighborhoods: Vernon Township was in considerable part settled by landless or land-poor children from Stillwater Township, and a considerable part of the population would have had parents, siblings, or cousins in Stillwater. Given the timing of births that Rhodes reports, the move could have taken place no later than 1847, so Rhodes would have been at most eight at the time. William Rhodes (1792–1853) was the author's adopted father's oldest brother and was, as the author later notes, a prosperous dairy farmer.

12   Alfred R. Toland (1841–1902) served as a corporal in Company F of the 27th New Jersey Volunteers, Rhodes's regiment; remaining in New Jersey, he pursued a variety of white-collar positions, including postmaster. Julia Toland Morehous (1839–1927) appears to have lived her entire life in the Glenwood area. Charles Arvis Crissey (1841–1915) served as a private in Company F of the 27th New Jersey Volunteers, becoming a banker in Warwick, NY, about eight miles from Glenwood. George Clark Crissey (born 1846) moved to Michigan. The Crissey boys were Rhodes's cousins on his adopted father's side. Charles J. Baxter (1841–1915) served as sergeant in Company F of the 27th New Jersey Volunteers; he became a teacher, high school principal, and superintendent of schools in Sussex County. Katherine Baxter (1842–1935) appears to have lived her life as a spinster in the Glenwood area. Daniel Bailey (born 1841) commanded Company F of the 27th New Jersey Volunteer Infantry; coming from a well-to-do family, he in turn became a prosperous

Brother Charles was born at North Vernon at Uncle William Rhodes' home.[13]

---

farmer, store-owner, entrepreneur, and political figure in Glenwood.

Rhodes's notes contain both an anecdote and an observation on technology that appear to relate to his time here in Glenwood. The anecdote provides insights into entertainment —and into the problems of finance and capital acquisition that were already a principal concern for him.

> "It was while living here I had my first pack of firecrackers. Mother seemed constitutionally opposed to such noises and would not furnish me with money to buy even one package of boy's delight. One Fourth the temptation seemed irresistible. We had a large flock of geese. My young pal George Crissey and I drove the geese a long distance from the house, corralled them in an old sheep pen, and proceeded quietly but vigorously to acquire barter for firecrackers by plucking quills, which were legal tender at the village store.
>
> That was a red letter Fourth of July for us. We did not then know that it had been declared aforetime that all men, including boys, are born with certain inalienable rights – among which is one to make a noise like war on July 4th. So we stole silently away to the woods and had our celebration alone. Small boys may be patriotic in their way, but are seldom diplomatic enough to hide their schemes from the home folk. So, in this case. Quilless geese gave our venture away, with the usual result where parents believe that to spare the rod is to spoil the child. The pain didn't last long, but the incidents of that day have been a pleasant memory even unto my old age."

Presumably triggered by the reference to geese quills, Rhodes's notes continued with an observation on quill pens and technological change:

> "When I commenced learning to write, there were no steel pens used in the schools – only goose quill pens. These needed attention every day or two. It was very common to hear, 'Teacher, please mend my pen,' which process consisted in cutting it back and forming a new point and slit. I remember my first steel pen very well. It was while at that school that Mother gave me money to buy one and how proud I was of it. It was a great annoyance to teachers to have to stop and mend pens. So, no doubt, all teachers became willing soliciting agents for Joseph Gillett's steel pens."

13   Lydia Ann Rhodes was probably born in 1845 and probably died in 1851 or 1852. Charles Predmore Rhodes (1847–1911) and his younger brother

After living here about three years, we moved to about a mile from Hamburg, Sussex County, and Father took the old Stoll flouring mill to run and we lived in a house just across the road from the mill. At the time I write, the mill is still standing, but the house is gone. Brother William was born here in Hamburg.[14]

In connection with this old mill is the following personal experience. A boy living perhaps a quarter of a mile from the mill and I were great chums and either would run away for a day and take a good whipping on coming home at night, rather than be deprived of the other's company. We rather gloried in the martyrdom we were enduring to be together and each cut a notch in a board, kept secreted for the purpose, when we got a whipping. So, in the rivalry as to whether Damon or Pythias had suffered most for friendship's sake, we would at times meet down in the thick hemlock woods below the mill with our boards and count notches, the one with the fewest would secretly resolve to suffer a whole lot rather than be behind at the next count. So much by way of introduction. One day Father had to attend

William Alva were orphaned at a young age—14 and 12—and were taken in by neighbors. They worked as canal laborers on the Chemung Canal until they reached their majority. Lured to Pennsylvania by the brief oil boom of 1869, "Charley" and "Will" began a peripatetic life that, with periodic assistance and interventions from Daniel Harker Rhodes to find them employment with railroads and to help them set up in trade, brought them wandering across Ohio and Michigan and eventually to Kansas and finally to Oklahoma.

14   William Alva Rhodes (1849–1920), like his brother Charley, held a variety of positions with railroads, typically arranged by Daniel Harker Rhodes, operated a number of stores and small retail businesses, and worked in local banking. Moving frequently, he and his family finally ended up in Hennessey, Oklahoma, where he lived the final 16 years of his life, dying a few months before Daniel Harker Rhodes.

a lawsuit at Hamburg. When he was ready to leave, he said, "Daniel, come over to the mill with me." As there was nothing unusual in the invitation, I went. Going down into the basement of the mill, Father unhooked the platform scales from the ring at the floor joist above and moved them away. Took a piece of rope I had not before noticed he had, passed it through the ring and standing me under it bound me securely in a standing position there in the middle of the floor. As he was going out of the door, he turned, looked me over and in a satisfied tone, said, "I will know where to find you this time when I return." I had no doubt about it—then. Soon as his carriage was out of hearing and my surprise and humiliation had abated a little, I realized that soon some customer would be coming for his milling and would surely find me. I could not bear the thought of such humiliation and commenced trying to get loose. I had worked fully an hour, had found the knot and loosened it, was practically free when the upper mill door opened and Mother appeared at the head of the stairs. The ropes were still around me, and I stood still. She expressed her sorrow that such was necessary with other appropriate remarks and waited. As the knot was loose and no one outside of the family had yet seen me, my reply was neither that of a penitent or a returning prodigal, so she left me and returned to the house. Had I shown the proper spirit, her Mother love and pride would then and there have found excuse for releasing me. But I did not feel that I needed her help just then, in fact, she was only delaying my departure. Soon as she was out of hearing, I threw off the ropes, let myself down into the cog pit to the great shaft that led to the overshot water wheel outside, crawled along the shaft to the outside, out on one of the great arms to the rim of the great wheel, reached around, got hold of the buckets and let myself down bucket by bucket into water up to my shoulders at the foot of the wheel and breathed again the air of freedom and though dripping from head to feet, felt the buoyancy of boyish delight natural under the circumstances. I soon put the mill between me and the house and in the shortest time possible was with my chum and helped him weed onions until night. I never told him I had been tied up though. Wouldn't have done it for the world! That was a family affair, besides there was something in my Mother's tones and look as she sat on the stairs that, in quiet moments of that day, made me feel uncomfortable. I could be mischievous, restless, and impatient of control, but never down deep, disloyal to Mother. From my earliest recollection she held me by a stronger tie than parental authority—love. Well, I reached home after dark that evening, sat down on a step of the porch and awaited developments that would surely call for another notch in my board. Both Father and Mother passed in and out but said not a word. This experience was as new and radical as that of the morning. I could not understand. My conscience demanded, and from an abundant experience, I had a right to expect a settlement before I went to bed. That day's account was never balanced corporally. I had no further use for my tally board. Both parents, in their extremity, had perhaps unknowingly, found the key to their boy's complete control.

The schoolhouse I attended here stood beside the road. Immediately back was a high ledge of jagged out-jutting rocks abounding in haw bushes, and in season we feasted on the berries. We knew them as "Nanny berries."[15] A short distance from the schoolhouse, on the opposite side of the road was the mill pond, a favorite resort for runaway schoolboys. This schoolhouse stood in a lonely place, rocks on one side, woods on the opposite, with no dwelling near, and, like many lonely places of that day, was a rendezvous for spirits, better known to us as witches. It was a daring boy or girl indeed who would pass the house alone at early evening. Not one of us would pass it after dark except with a grown person and then with many misgivings and side glances. Occasionally, when the witches would be reported as having been very active, and unusual movements, lights, and noises had been noticed in the building, a few of us boys would go quietly down the road toward the house and when within sight of it would hide in the rocks or bushes and watch. The rays from the setting sun, the reflection from the sunset clouds or the early moon, would often lighten up the windows of the old house with weird and ever-changing lights. If we happened to be watching at such a time, on the following day we could raise the hair and almost paralyze with fear the more timid scholars, as well as ourselves, with an almost breathless account of how the witches lighted up the house with their lights, and held high carnival there last night. After such times

---

15   Presumably *Vibernum lentago* or *Vibernum prunifolium.*

scholars going to school would wait on the way for the teacher to get to the house first, and there was no loitering about after school closed for the day, at least by the younger children. There was a small entrance room or hall in the schoolhouse where dinners and wraps were left on shelves or hooks. In the floor of this entry, near one side, was a very large knot hole. Often at noon when the presence of the teacher, most of the scholars, and daylight made us brave, we would get long sticks, run them down this hole and try to punch the witches under the floor. Sometimes the stick would catch. Then the bravest would fear. Why not, when some mysterious phantom under the floor was holding it?

On the main road to Hamburg and at the head of our mill race was a country store, kept by a Mr. Stoll. It was a favorite loitering place for me, as I passed it going to and coming from school. As I remember now, specie payment must have been in suspension at that time. Barter was legal tender, and as candy was more necessary to complete a small boy's happiness then than now, I bartered eggs for candy. One egg for one stick of candy. It was just as easy with two eggs to get two sticks of boy's delight—a progression in desire not uncommon to grown people. In a little while I was a traveling confection shop, admired of most of the small girls, an envied rival of most of the boys, who for revenge told my parents. They had been wondering where the eggs went, and Father had made two box traps and kept them setting about to catch the minx or rats that were carrying off all the eggs. Barter and I were out. The cloud, as usual, had a gilded lining, however, for about this time Father had an idea. He secured a large store box. For the tight bottom he substituted slats, set it under the side waste gate of the long wooden flume leading to the great overshot wheel. After he had shut down the mill in the evening, he would raise the waste gate and let the water flow into his improvised weir all night. In the morning when the gate was shut down, what a sight there was in that box for a boy! Dozens of monster eels large around as a man's arm, a crawling, squirming, writhing, slimy mass. There was fish and to spare. So father would give me the catfish and all others but the eels. Then business with me was good again. I bartered fish for candy, was restored to favor with my former little admirers, and as cordially envied by their would-be favorites.

It was while living here near Hamburg that I attended my first circus. Father could hardly *spare the time*, but like the kind parent he was, denied himself the pleasure of working one afternoon and took me to the circus. Such sights! Mardi Gras, carnivals, Veiled Prophets and pageants, the pomp of war, Phoebus driving his flaming steeds along the clouds with sun rays for his highway, the feats of India's trained jugglers and of Japan's world famous balancers, all these pale before the memory of that show! Indeed Macaulay's New Zealander shall sit upon a crumbling tower of London Bridge and sketch the ruins of St. Paul's ere I shall see its like again.[16]

---

16   The reference is to a remark by Thomas Babington Macauley regarding the endurance of the Roman Catholic Church in his essay "Ranke's History of the Popes," which appeared in *The Edinburgh Review* in October 1840. As with many of Rhodes's literary references, there is no clear relationship to the context of the original.

I attended church and Sabbath School at Hamburg. Gov. Haines, who lived there, was a teacher in our Sabbath School.[17]

Brother William A. Rhodes was born while we lived here. As I remember, we only lived near Hamburg about a year, then moved to the Kimball place about a mile from Unionville, New York.[18] Father ran the Kimball Flouring Mill. Our house was a story and a half above a full basement. The basement was entered on the ground level. The main floor, the same, as the ground about the house was sloping. It stood beside the main road where it skirted the mill pond, and was but a stone's throw from the pond. It was just about a mile from the house to the main part of Unionville, N.Y. In this house Brother George Marcus Rhodes was born and Sister Lydia Ann died.[19] She was about six

17   Daniel Haines (1801–1877), a Hamburg resident and attorney practicing in Hamburg and Newton (the county seat of Sussex County), served as Governor of New Jersey from 1843 to 1845, and from 1848 to 1851. From 1852 to 1866 he served as an Associate Justice on the New Jersey Supreme Court. Haines's father was a wealthy New York merchant and his mother came from a prominent New Jersey family—his maternal uncle, Aaron Ogden served as governor in 1812–1813. Haines was educated at Princeton, and was a major reformer in New Jersey politics, championing a new constitution, educational reform, and prison reform.

18   The hamlet of Unionville, Orange County, New York lies aside the New York-New Jersey state line, 12 miles directly north from Hamburg, New Jersey and roughly seven miles northwest from Glenwood. While part of New York State for legal purposes, demographically and topographically Unionville was part of Sussex County, New Jersey. Rhodes's comment regarding William Alva's birth suggests the move from Hamburg to Unionville would have taken place some time in 1850; his later suggestion that the family stayed there only a year before moving on again in 1853 would suggest a date of 1852. Presumably the move occurred at some point in that time window.

19   George Marcus Rhodes (about 1853–1887), the baby of the

or seven years old, died of brain fever and was buried in private grounds on Uncle William Rhodes' farm in North Vernon. The grave is beside the main road, left hand side, going from the house toward the barn and probably forty rods from the house. Sister was an unusually bright girl in her studies. She was the only girl Mother ever had and her loss so affected her she never seemed to recover from the shock.

I attended school in the village most of the time (and there I loitered when I had letters for Father), and had no thrilling adventures or hair-breadth escapes. I think we lived here for about one year, for in the spring of 1853, the family moved to Pine Valley, Chemung County, New York.[20] I stayed with Uncle

family, was separated from his brothers after they were all orphaned and was raised by his half-sister Mary Rhodes McSchooler, their father's daughter by his first marriage. George lived his life in the Finger Lakes region of New York State, rejoining his brothers Charley and Will in Cairo, Kansas only when he was dying of tuberculosis.

20   Pine Valley is a crossroads roughly four miles north of Horseheads, New York, and three miles south of Millport on present-day Route 14, at the southern end of the Finger Lakes region. As a crow flies, the move from Unionville to Pine Valley was one of about 130 miles, or about 180 miles by road. This was the first time that the family moved outside a circle with a diameter of 25 miles, from what Swartswood at the southwestern end of Sussex County, New Jersey, to Glenwood at the northeastern end. The family's move from Sussex County, New Jersey to Chemung County, New York was part of a general move from Sussex County to that part of New York: a substantial number of landless, land-poor, underemployed, or restless offspring of Sussex County's prolific parents had made this trek (just as their grandparents had made the trek from Monmouth County, New Jersey to Sussex County, and their parents had moved from southwestern Sussex County to northeastern Sussex County). In making this move, Rhodes's family was "catching up" with relatives who had already made the jump, rather than charting new territory. The move was presumably made with an eye to Rhodes's adopted father's advancing age and anticipated infirmity. John Rhodes's brother George had settled in Corning, New York,

William Rhodes until late fall then followed them to Pine Valley. It was during this summer that I learned to milk. Uncle had about thirty milch cows and all—men and women—old enough had to milk.

In the herd was a farrow cow and she was assigned to me to practice upon. It was no small thing to have a reputation as a good milker in that great dairy country—Sussex County, New Jersey and the neighboring Orange, New York. It was worth striving for and often meant a situation. Realizing this I determined the cow should not fail in her milk while I was the operator. On the sly she got many an extra feed, and by getting a little water in my pail often, I succeeded in keeping her quantity of milk rather above what was expected.

In about a month my reputation as a milker warranted them in assigning me two more cows. At the time I was very proud of being considered a journeyman milker; in time, however, it become so burdensome I lost interest in the reputation. Especially when it reached the limit of eight cows each night and morning, my Aunt *kindly* dropping out.[21]

What an amount of work those large dairy's [sic] made for the house folks, especially. The churning was done by

---

some 18 miles west of Pine Valley, probably in the 1830s, and one of John Rhodes's sons and two of his daughters by his first marriage had settled in Millport, at least as early as 1838. Presumably one of his sons-in-law, who was employed by the railroad, arranged the retirement job in Pine Valley.

21   As prominently as modes of production and technology figure in Rhodes's recollections and various writings, equally noticeable by their infrequency are references to human relationships and to death. At about the same time Rhodes began milking eight cows, his uncle William—the man to whom the cows belonged and in whose home Rhodes was living—died. The uncle's death and the upheaval it must have caused in the household were apparently much less memorable than the problems of turning a treadmill.

an animal of some kind. Some using a calf; some, a colt; a sheep, or a dog. We used a large dog. He traveled upon a circular platform or wheel ten or twelve feet or more in diameter, standing at quite an angle. Usually two churns were run at a time, each larger than a barrel. In midsummer, we often had to churn twice. The dog did not like the treadmill any better than a boy would, and whenever he could, would hide out. If he was not found in time, the boy would have to take his place unless a substitute animal was at hand. On this particular farm boy meant myself, and many were the times I trod the butter from the milk, sweating vengeance on the dog at every pore. That wheel was to me like Sysiphus rolling his stone, ever climbing but never advancing. From a distance dim and long I forgive that dog, for hiding out was akin to the human. Not to have done so was only dumb brute.

Not later than 5 A.M. the churns were started and there was no sleep after that hour for worker, drone or queen. There was always slack motion enough in the machinery to fill the morning with indescribable sounds. The varying pitch, quality, and volume of screeches from dry journals, the clattering grind of the cog wheels, the chuckety-chuck-chuck of loose pins, the panting of the dog as he hung back until almost choked, the "Go on Carlo," no there was no sleep after 5 A.M.

The butter was packed into new clean and sweet oak firkins [ed: a small cask with a volume of about 41 liters], made upon honor at the village cooper-shop. They were hooped with one-half inch hickory hoops cut from the neighboring woods and driven well to place to the familiar sound of cooperdang, cooperdang, cooperdang. When these were filled, they were covered with a well-brined white muslin cloth and ranged along one side of the cool, moist cellar. Each good housewife must show up two full firkins of butter for each cow, or have a good reason why. During Autumn Sabbaths after church and before Sunday School, the housewives would get together and compare notes, not so often upon the sermon as on the state of the dairy and the number of firkins in their cellars, the number of cows, the increase or decrease of milk on account of good or poor pastures. If any there were somewhat short of the maximum number of firkins, such would cut the discussion short and join in a stroll through the burying ground surrounding the church on three sides. Epitaphs were more to their liking than the arrowed questions of their more fortunate or more industrious neighbors.[22]

---

22   In his notes for the manuscript, Rhodes provides additional information on the practicalities of home economics in his youth:

> "Late in the fall the surplus apples, potatoes, cabbage, and edible roots were buried in the ground for late winter use. In a place where water would not stand, one or more holes would be dug, each from six inches to a foot in depth and in diameter about four feet, varying with the amount of produce to be buried. The hole was thickly lined with long rye straw that had been threshed with a flail. Upon this straw was placed and coned up as high as they would stand whatever was to be buried. Then covered with straw and that with earth perhaps six inches or more thick. For current use of this buried stuff, a hole that would barely admit the hand and arm was made in one side. This hole when not in use was kept carefully covered over. It was a cheap cold storage plant, and very seldom did fruit or vegetables freeze if properly buried."

In the pre-electricity era, light as well as refrigeration was a challenge resolved through advance planning and the application of the technology and raw materials at hand.

> "After beef killing in the fall and before the long evenings of winter came on the thrifty housewife prepared to supplement the cheerful glow of the old fireplace by making a supply of tallow candles. The following was the process: Purchase a sufficient supply of candle wicking. This

came in balls. Procure a quantum sufficient of wooden rods about two feet long, about one-half inch in diameter and smooth. Place a couple of chairs four to six feet apart. With ends resting upon these chairs lay two poles parallel to support the above rods. Cut wicking twice the length of the candle to be; double it over a rod, bring the ends even and twist them into one strand. Do this six or eight times with each of as many rods as the poles will hold with the rods spaced about three or four inches apart. Melt a good supply of tallow in an ordinary wash boiler. Pour in hot water until the melted tallow stands as near the top of the boiler as practicable without running over. The rods having been spaced as above on the poles, pick up a rod, dip the wicking into the tallow until the rod rests upon the top of the boiler. Remove it and place it upon the poles, the embryo candle hanging from the rod. The strands of wicking being placed near together on the rods will often adhere to each other on coming from their dip. Separate them by running the finger down between them. Repeat this process for all the rods upon the poles. Then commence at No. 1 again. Continue dipping until enough of the tallow has been taken up by the strands of the wicking to make a candle of the desired size for domestic use.

The boiler must be kept full up all the time or there will be too long a neck to the finished candle. When the candles have hardened, slip them off the rods and pack away for future use. Repeat the whole process until the number of candles required are made.

Another method was to use candle moulds. The moulds or forms were made of tin in the shape and size of the candle to be. These moulds were soldered together in any number desired from a 2-candle to a 144-candle. Poor people mostly used these, as they could make a few candles any time they happened to have a little tallow or grease on hand. A wick suspended from a rod resting upon the rim around the top of the mould was passed down through the mould. This wick just filled the conical tip and prevented the melted tallow from running through. This tip held the wick in the center of the to-be-candle at the bottom, and it was adjusted to the center on top. When all was ready, tallow was poured in to fill the mould, and set away to cool. To remove the now finished candles, warm the mould a little and withdraw them.

Through the system of lending and borrowing so convenient and universal, one or two sets of moulds would answer for a whole settlement.

A more primitive light, a cheap substitute for the candle often used in the kitchen, was a saucer (perhaps) of most any kind of grease, some wicking or a piece of muslin, one end of which lay upon the

The staff of life among the best farmers, as among the poorer, was rye bread. Usually made in large loves and baked in a brick oven. As I remember, this was better and more nutritious than our present (1900) refined wheat bread. More rye than wheat was raised as it was good feed for both man and beast. There was always wheat flour in the house, but it took a preacher or a much-honored visitor to get it moulded into bread or biscuits. Even in such an event the plate of rye bread was in evidence and there was an unwritten rule or understanding that the farm men were to *prefer* rye to wheat. I have seen a plate of luscious biscuits pass the gauntlet of a half dozen farm hands without any being taken, but, oh how everyone of them wanted a half dozen! At communion time when some one would bring loves of white bread all cut into such nice little cubes, we boys would seriously consider whether it would not be worth joining the church to get a taste of that nice wheat bread.[23]

---

rim of the dish just out of the oil. This would burn until the oil or grease was all gone. From these to the electric light is the seemingly fabulous progress in lighting in the ordinary lifetime.

With the candle went the plain or ornamental candlestick and a pair of iron snuffers to remove the charred wick. Woe to the one who snuffed the candle with shears; the charred wick would surely fall and leave its tell-tale mark. While one lighted candle would but little more than make the darkness visible, two was mostly considered an extravagance."

23   Rhodes's notes provide insights into some of the other luxuries of the day as well, and into the technology of making the everyday items. Observe (in the final paragraph of this note) the multiple uses and opportunities that this technology provided for the entrepreneurial child....

"In my childhood days hard soap was somewhat of a luxury, and with wheat biscuits was reserved for Sunday and other (holiday) scrubs known now as *baths*. Each housewife made or superintended

My Uncle was one of the thrifty and wealthy farmers of that section, and their ways and living was above rather than below the average. We raised and killed our own meat of every kind, cut all our grain with a cradle and gathered it with a hand rake and during winters threshed it all with

---

the making of her [everyday] soap. Wood was the only fuel known, and wood ashes were necessary in soap-making.

The 'lye gum' was a hogshead or a section of a hollow gum tree, probably the latter as it would not warp and twist as hogshead staves would. The section would be about six feet long. Inside, about two feet in diameter. Both ends were left open, but it stood upon a slanting board high enough from the ground to set a pail under the board. A layer of boulders were put in the gum. Upon this layer some twigs and straw were placed, then the gum was filled with wood ashes. At frequent intervals water was poured upon the ashes, and in due time the liquid ran from the gum as lye.

If the lye was not strong enough to float an egg, it was poured back into the gum and less water used until the egg would float. The perennial joke among soap makers was this one: An old lady was once describing the process to a city visitor. When she came to the matter of the strength of the lye, she hesitated but finally said that it must be strong enough to float an egg or not to float it, really she had forgotten which!

Any old fat and grease that had been accumulated for the purpose was now put in a big iron kettle over an outside fire, lye poured in and stirred, mind you, with a sassafras stick, until of the proper consistency when it was turned into the soap barrel. This process was repeated until sufficient supply of soft soap was accumulated for a year's supply. The grease and lye that went into the big iron kettle came out as soft soap. Flesh was scarcely safe with that soap when it was *new*, but age modified its biting abrasive quality somewhat. Still soft soap and hard rubbing on the washboard would usually bring blood on the knuckles each Monday morning. The hands of the housewives of that day were rough and harsh.

When we boys had captured a ground hog [i.e., woodchuck], we would put wet ashes on the skin until the hair came off. Then surreptitiously we would sink the skin to the bottom of the barrel of soap to cure or tan the hide. Sometimes the soap would be low and the periodical stirring with the sassafras stick would reveal the tanning process. Then we would be candidates for a tanning."

a flail. The straw was better to cut for horse feed and for other purposes. The mowing was done with a scythe and mostly raked by hand. We had one revolving rake, but few were used. Harvesters were unknown. Mowers were talked of by those who traveled quite extensively.

On December 25th [1853] I reached the Valley [that is, Pine Valley, New York] I was fifteen years old. In 1852 I helped drive some cattle from home [Unionville, New York] to Port Jervis, N.Y. and saw railroad, cars, and canal boats for the first time.[24] I had never seen anything on the water as large as a canal boat and was interested when I saw people go down in the cabin, apparently right down in the water. As for the railroad tracks in the yard about the depot, before crossing anything that looked like a track, I watched both ways then jumped. If there were several tracks together, I think I jumped them all at once if it was possible. About the first thing, when I was at liberty, I went to the depot. While standing on the platform, a train came up. I got opposite the engine and was taking the strange and formidable-looking thing in, when it whistled. I went up some distance. When I got down, I saw people laughing, and so went around the depot out of sight and communed with myself. Afterwards *I* became a railroad man.

Cousin George W. Dodder kept the Deer Park Hotel

---

24   Port Jervis, New York, is on the Delaware River, at the point where New York, New Jersey, and Pennsylvania meet. The distance from Unionville is only about 12 miles. The Delaware and Hudson Canal, passing through Port Jervis, was completed in 1828; the railroad opened in 1847 and the line was completed in 1851. Port Jervis was thus at the time an important terminus for commercial shipment of agricultural produce. Rhodes would have been 13 ½-years old at this time.

and I stayed with them while there.[25] When I came West [i.e., when he joined his family in Pine Valley, Chemung County, New York in 1853], I took the train at Goshen[26] for Elmira and Millport, and that was the first time I was ever on a railroad train. Railroads were not as common in 1852 as in 1900.

On my return home from Port Jervis I had traveled and was "Sir Oracle" on the subject of railroads, the way the trains moved, canals and their crafts, the ways of city life and "sic." Father and Mother used to encourage me to give them over and again my observations on that trip. Then would have a hearty laugh. I did not realize then what pleased them so, but the older one grows, the more he finds "by gracious oudt."

At Pine Valley Father worked for the Canandagua and Elmira Railroad (now the Northern Central) as bridge watchman on a long trestle with trussed spans over the two canal crossings, the whole extending entirely across and over the Valley. It was a long and very important bridge. He purchased a home just across the road from the village schoolhouse and at the foot of the hill where the road went up the mountain. That was home; we were all together, comfortable and pleasantly situated. The home circle was complete except for Sister Lydia. How little we know of even the immediate future!

---

25   This is the same cousin George Dodder who had kept the public house in Swartswood. Like others, he was moving on in search of better business opportunities. Three years later, in 1855, Dodder made the big jump and moved much further west, to Iowa City, Iowa; his historical claim to fame is that as justice of the peace in 1869 he empaneled what some records suggest may have been the first jury of African Americans. In the present context, however, note the importance of extended family in facilitating travel.

26   Goshen, New York: roughly 15 miles northeast of Unionville.

During the summers of 1854, 5, and 6 I worked at various places; on a farm near Horseheads, one summer; another, with John Rhodes, near Townsend Settlement to learn the millwright trade.[27] One hot summer day he set me to sawing off seasoned elm timbers intended for arms to a large overshot water wheel. After two or three days I had learned all I cared to know about the millwright business but stayed with him through the summer.

During these summers I could get home every few Sundays, and no boy ever endured more to get home than I did. I would start from Horseheads Saturday evening or early Sunday morning and walk to Pine Valley, to be home only a few hours, then walk back, and feel amply repaid.

Mother was on active duty about the home at this time, but her health and strength were not vigorous. She was failing. The loss of her only daughter, the care of a young child (George), the journey from Unionville to Pine Valley, the hard work and exposure in getting settled in the new home, together with the daily work and care for a family consisting of Father, Mother, myself, Charles, Will, and baby George, was more a burden than she could bear. She caught cold before I left home for Aurora, and she had lung trouble, terrible coughing attacks, and days when she would

---

27   This John Rhodes (born 1824) was Rhodes's nominal step-brother—he was the eldest surviving son of Rhodes's adopted father, John Rhodes, by his first marriage. Townsend was a crossroads several miles west of Watkins Glen, New York, where Townsend Road intersects Montour-Townsend—about 12 miles northwest of Pine Valley. A millwright was a specialized carpenter with the practical engineering skills required to build a mill. Rhodes's parents were trying to find a calling that suited him.

be sick in bed from exhaustion.[28] She was making the true wife and mother's sacrifice for her loved ones, giving her life, none the less truly but more heroic, that the mental anxiety and physical suffering was prolonged. She continued getting worse and in the summer of 1857 she wrote me (then at Aurora) she thought if she could go East and visit her relatives and friends in Sussex County, New Jersey, the change and relief from household cares might enable her to gain her strength again. Father could not well leave his work and the younger children, so I came to Pine Valley and went East with her. We went to a relative (Cousin Hunt's) in Troy, Pa., for a few days.[29] Then to Cousin Jacob Predmore's in Montague, N.J., a farmer living near the "Brick House" Hotel.[30] She stopped here to rest and visit. She could scarcely sit up all day and required constant care and nourishment on the trip East. She would talk of the cross it was to leave her children, but hoped to gain strength and better health that she might do more for them when

---

28   This would have been in October 1856; Aurora is about 55 miles north of Pine Valley, on the eastern shore of Cayuga Lake. As explained later, Rhodes made the move there to learn the tinsmith trade. Although Rhodes is discreet in not making reference to his mother's illness, other family members in their records were candid regarding the diagnosis: tuberculosis.

29   Troy, Pennsylvania is 35 miles directly south from Pine Valley. "Cousin Hunt" was presumably William P. Hunt (born 1806), who was married to Eliza Ann Predmore (born 1815), one of Margaret Ann's second cousins and presumably a childhood playmate.

30   Jacob C. Predmore (1816–1890) was the eldest son of Margaret Ann's brother Daniel Harker Predmore, the head of the Predmore family at this time. Montague Township, Sussex County, New Jersey lies along the Delaware River south of Port Jervis and about 17 miles north of Swartswood/New Patterson. The Brick House Hotel was located where Route 206 crosses the Delaware River to Milford, Pennsylvania. A local landmark built in 1776, the Hotel was razed in 1953 to accommodate road-widening.

she returned home. She took with her what she thought she might need and a few keepsake reminders of home.

I left her at Cousin Jacob Predmore's. He was Uncle Daniel Predmore's (Mother's brother) son, and returned to Aurora. They took her to her Brother Daniel's near New Patterson and from there she visited, as her strength would permit, relatives and friends thereabout. With the approach of winter she was worse, and was finally confined to the house at Uncle Daniel's. Uncle Daniel's daughter Mary Moore and her daughter Jane, a young lady, were living at Uncle Daniel's and gave Mother tender and loving care.[31] At this time I received in Mother's handwriting the following:

Dear Son:

I hope you are well. I must tell you that my strength is failing fast. I am not able to sit up longer than to have my bed made. I have things as comfortable as possible. I have moved upstairs in the room where you slept. I have been around visiting most of the time, have not been here but about four weeks. I would like to see you, but traveling is so expensive I hardly dare ask you to come. I waited to get a letter from Millport [Pine Valley: that is, from her husband, John Rhodes] but have got none yet.... A word more to you, my son. Don't forget to serve the Lord. You will not be sorry. It will fit you to live and it will fit you to die, and it is the

---

31   Mary Effie Predmore Moore (born 1821) was presumably the widow of Robert Moore at this time. The reference in Rhodes's mother's letter to "the room where you slept" would suggest the possibility that they were staying in Margaret Ann Predmore Rhodes's former home in Swartswood.

only thing that can make you really happy. I was about 16 years old when I sought religion and am not sorry yet. I will close now, hoping you will remember my request.

—Margaret A. Rhodes

December 29, 1857, she wrote me, in part, as follows:

Dear Son:

I received your kind letter Christmas evening, pleased to hear that you were well.... I want you to come soon after the holidays. I think that Mr. Winch will spare you then. My strength is failing so fast that you may not have an opportunity of seeing me long.... Your Uncle read your letter to me. I was not able to sit up.... You will pardon me for writing little, for I have to take it on my bed and a chair at my back while I write.

—Margaret A. Rhodes

In January, 1858, they sent me word I must come at once if I would see her before she passed away. Soon as possible I started East. Reached Uncle Daniel's about noon. Mother was entirely conscious, talked with me in a whisper, from weakness, and seemed so relieved and content at having seen and embraced me, that after an hour or so, she took little note of anything except to smile or gently press my hand in response to my caress.

She passed away that evening (February 8, 1858—Aged 47 yrs. 7 mos, 27 days). They had been looking for it for a week or more, but she told them she could not go until she had seen me, and she lived about eight hours after her desire was gratified. We buried her at Swartsood Cemetary.

My Mother was my idol. My love for her, consuming and after a lapse of 40 years and at the age of seventy-three, I cannot even write the few words I have without a choking heart and blinding tears.[32] She died as she had lived, a member of the Presbyterian Church, a devoted, loving Christian wife and Mother.

In October, 1856, I had left home for good. I went with Walter Winch at Aurora, New York, to learn the tin and hardware business. I remained there through the spring of 1860.

---

32   As in multiple places in the text, there is evidence here that this was rewritten or revised a number of times, over a period from roughly 1900 to 1911. The "lapse of 40 years" is roughly consistent with the 1900 date of the manuscript; the "age of seventy-three" implies that this passage was a later emendation to the manuscript, authored in 1911 or possibly 1912.

It is dangerous to read too much into limited information, but the relationship between 20-year-old Rhodes and his mother—and, indeed, between the whole family and her—may not have been quite as close or intense as remembered or reported in later life. Note that, by Rhodes's own account, he needed to be summoned at least three times (the last time by "them" — presumably his uncle and namesake, the *pater familias* of the Predmore clan) before he left work to come to his mother's deathbed. Note, too, that Rhodes seems to have deposited his mother rather unceremoniously with her nephew at the first family habitation in New Jersey. And finally note also his mother's complaint that she had heard nothing at all from her husband or younger children. Son William, who would have been eight at the time of his mother's death, later in life wrote that he thought that she had "died at her father's home" (indeed, not an unreasonable confusion given the father-like role that Daniel Harker Predmore had played in his much younger sister's life, but also suggesting that he had had no significant contact with his mother's family after her death) and candidly admitted that she was buried "at some place in New Jersey, now forgotten by me."

Thoroughly learned the trade and business under a thorough mechanic. I was well equipped to do for myself. My compensation while there was $50.00 for the first year, $60.00 for the second, and $80 for the third, board, room, washing, and mending in his family. He had a good store, the only hardware house in the place, a good business. A well-to-do Christian family. I had to attend church and Sabbath School with the family regularly. Had a pleasant home, with elevating influences; did my whole duty; was ever after honored with the warm and active friendship of the whole family and gave them the same in return. That was a character-forming period of my life—18 to 21 years—and I was fortunate in my immediate surroundings. I had never seen much of the great world, having lived at home and mostly in rural districts. I was undeveloped, shy to timidity, slow and cautious in forming friendships, but prizing beyond measure friendships once formed.

I had the confidence and respect of young and old, but was not intimate or as—one might now express it—"chummy" with either, except an occasional friend. There always seemed to be an indefinable, but none the less impassable, barrier between myself and those I mingled with. This has followed me through life…. [ed.: ellipses in original text.]

Father continued to live at the Valley home with my younger brothers until failing health compelled him to break up the home and live with one of his daughters by a previous wife, Mary McSchooler of Millport, New York.[33] By this time the family were scattered away never

---

33   Mary Rhodes McSchooler (1821–1894) was the third of six children of John Rhodes by his first wife, Mary Shackelton. Her husband, William McSchooler, was a railroad employee and had presumably facilitated John Rhodes's retirement job as a railroad bridge-tender.

to be united again in one home. God grant that we may again all be united in the Home beyond! Father was tenderly nursed and cared for, but his trouble, dropsy, could not be cured, and on March, 1861, he, too, passed away, and was laid to rest in the Millport cemetery.[34]

As before stated, I remained at Aurora until the early spring of 1860. Then I went to Deckertown, New Jersey, and worked at my business for Mr. Samuel T. Overhiser.[35] Mr. Overhiser had married a Miss Stoddard, daughter of Increase and Mariah Stoddard, who owned and lived on a farm about four miles from Deckertown on the road to Newton. They [ed.: that is, the Stoddards] had a family of, if I remember, eleven children. As I lived at Overhiser's, I soon became acquainted with most of the family, with all in fact, except one. Nelson and Lucy Stoddard being near my age, I was most intimate with.[36] Nelson being then a merchant in Deckertown, unmarried

---

34   There is insufficient information to make any very certain diagnosis, but from the description it is plausible that John Rhodes was suffering from edema due to congestive heart failure. There is no indication in the record that Daniel Harker Rhodes returned to Millport for his adopted father's final days or funeral or was involved in any way in the decisions about what was to be done with younger brothers, Charles, William, and George.

35   Deckertown, in Sussex County, is now known as Sussex, New Jersey. A prosperous farm town, it was close to the various Sussex County locations where Rhodes grew up: 5 miles from Hamburg, 8 miles from Unionville, 9 miles from Glenwood, 16 miles from Swartswood. Samuel T. Overhiser (1825–1882) was a tinsmith.

36   Nelson Stoddard (born 1838) was one of 10 children. Following his Civil War service— he was a Sergeant in Rhodes's company of the 27th New Jersey Volunteers and one of Rhodes's usual tent-mates—Stoddard ran a store in Deckertown before taking a position as an accountant with the Erie Railroad and later becoming a postmaster and a banker. Lucy Stoddard was born in 1840 and, as Rhodes recounts later, died in 1897.

and living at Overhiser's, we soon became fast friends and companions and were nearly always together in the events that occurred in Deckertown society. Parties, singing schools, concerts, choirs, etc. With his sister Lucy I was but little less familiar. The family were all staunch Methodists, while I was Presbyterian by choice, but not by profession. However as Nelson and I sang in both choirs and attended choir meetings at both churches, and Lucy always played the organ at the Methodist Church, we were often together. I mention this here because after 36 years of separation and when Lucy had been 14 years the widow of George Coe (who, after Nelson Stoddard, was my most intimate friend in Deckertown), Lucy became my wife. She married George W. Coe on January 15, 1863.[37]

I continued with Overhiser until September, 1862. The Civil War having broken out in April, 1861, the struggle had become so fierce, the lines between those for and against the War, so sharply drawn in every community that those in sympathy with the North and who could, felt it a patriotic duty to go into the Army. So on September 1, 1862, I volunteered and went out in Company H, 27th New Jersey Volunteers under Colonel Mindil and Captain Samuel Dennis of Deckertown.[38] The Company was raised mostly in and about Deckertown, and I knew

---

37   George W. Coe (born 1841) owned and operated a foundry in Deckertown. Coe seems to be one of the relatively few in his age cohort who did not enlist for Civil War service. His marriage to Lucy occurred while Rhodes was away in the Army, though he clearly recalls the date.

38   In his notes, Rhodes observes: "My first Pres. vote was for A. Lincoln. My father was democrat & so was I [prior to the Civil War]." Rhodes kept a contemporaneous diary of his Civil War service. Omitted from this and from all of other accounts of his service is that he enlisted as a "fifer"— that is, as a musician rather than a regular soldier.

a majority of the members. We went into camp at Camp Frelinghuysen two and one-half miles from Newark. October 11, we left the Camp and on the morning of the 12th were in Washington, coming via Philadelphia and Baltimore. We went into regimental camp on East Capitol Hill (Camp Kearney) near the Emory Hospital. October 28 we left camp and marched to Fairfax Seminary and camped. The regiment did picket duty here until December 1st when we broke camp, marched to and through Washington and on to a Smith's Point, where we took the transport "Long Branch" to Acquia Creek.[39] Snow, rain, and mud. More than 100 vessels lying in the Bay. December 10, we reach the Army encamped north of the River opposite Fredericksburg, Maryland [sic: Virginia]. Early on the morning of December 12, 1862, we cross the Rappahannock into the city, and are decidedly "in it." The battle of Fredericksburg being in

---

George Washington Mindil (1841–1907) was already a distinguished war hero at the time he was given command of the 27th New Jersey; after the 27th New Jersey disbanded, Mindil received further commissions and saw more intense fighting, finishing the war as a Brevet Major General. After the war he became a jeweler in New York City. Samuel Dennis (1824–1891) was a merchant in Deckertown.

39   Camp Frelinghuysen, a major mustering-in and training facility, was located roughly in the area that is now Newark's Branch Brook Park. Emory Hospital was one of the many temporary hospitals established in Washington during the war. It was located near the Congressional Cemetery, between Capitol Hill and the Anacostia River. The Fairfax Episcopal Seminary— now the Theological Seminary of Virginia, in Alexandria —was a major base and hospital during the Civil War. Smith's Point and nearby Liverpool Point, where Rhodes's contemporaneous notes indicate the embarkation actually took place, are in Nanjemoy, Maryland, on the Potomac south of Washington. Aquia Creek Landing, Virginia, is just across the wide Potomac from Nanjemoy. As the terminus of the Richmond, Fredericksburg, & Potomac railroad, Aquia Creek served as a principal base for various Union campaigns against Richmond. In November 1862, the commander of the Union Army of the Potomac, General Ambrose Burnsides, rebuilt it as a base of operations.

Above: Daniel Harker Rhodes at age 17.

Above: Margaret Ann Predmore, Daniel Harker Rhodes's mother.

John Rhodes, Daniel Harker Rhodes's adopted father.

William Alva ("Will") Rhodes,
Daniel Harker Rhodes's brother.

Ida Rhodes, Will Rhodes's wife.

Portrait of Daniel Harker Rhodes's immediate family. Back row (left to right): Anna Rhodes, wife of Charles Predmore ("Charley") Rhodes; Ida Rhodes, wife of Will Rhodes. Middle row (left to right): Daniel Harker Rhodes's brother Charley Rhodes; Daniel Harker Rhodes's brother Will Rhodes. Front row (left to right): Will Rhodes's son Charles Harker Rhodes; Will Rhodes's son Harry Herbert Rhodes. Photo taken in mid-1880s, at the time the families relocated to Kansas with Daniel Harker Rhodes's assistance.

Store operated by Charley and Will Rhodes in Cairo, Kansas, in the late 1880s. In the carriage: Will and Ida Brown Rhodes. Pulling the carriage: "Old Kit." Boys at right: Charles Harker and Harry Rhodes. Dog at their feet: "Old Ben."

Above: Daniel Harker Rhodes, about 1920. At left, Daniel Harker Rhodes's second wife, Mattie Youkey Rhodes. At right, Daniel Harker Rhodes's sister-in-law Ida Rhodes.

progress. After dark on December 15 we silently "steal" away and recross the River. The pontoon bridges had been liberally sanded to silence the noise of crossing. We marched back to our old camp of five days ago and where we had stacked everything but guns, ammunition, blankets, and a few rations.[40]

40   At Fredericksburg, the 27th New Jersey was part of the Second (Christ's) Brigade of the First (Burns's) Division of the Ninth (Wilcox's) Corps, which was assigned to General Edwin Sumner's "Grand Right Division" for the assault. Burns's Division had the good fortune to be placed on the extreme right of the Union line, which may explain how the 27th New Jersey escaped the bloodbath of Fredericksburg without a single fatality— and, indeed, finished its nine months without a single battle death. Rhodes's contemporaneous diary chronicles the terrible days of Fredericksburg thus:

"Dec 11th. This Morning at 5 ock [o'clock] the ball opens and Fredericksburg is being bombarded. all are up and wide awake as it is the first realities we have heard. We have orders to pile our knapsacks at Camp and at 8 all are in line and March quarter of a Mile and are halted and lay [on] our arms all day. the whole Brigade is the same. the Bombardment continues all day without intermission. 3 ock Fredericksburg is on fire and will probably be reduced to ashes. the day clear and Moderately warm. at 6 we March to the river but go back without crossing and encamp for the Night. there is no cannonading since dusk.

Dec 12th. This Morning we are on the road at 5 Minutes Notice without any breakfast. March down to the river and at 9 ock cross the Rappahannock into the citty of Fredericksburg. there is heavy cannonading. one Mile up the river we cross without any opposition and Stop in line just over the Stream and Stay there until through the day. 4 ock while i am writing, there is a heavy cannonading going on on every side. Shots whizing over our heads every few Minutes. the rebs lay 2 Miles back of the town. the town is a perfect desolation. the houses are deserted and the Soldiers are reveling in booty. there is hardly a house that has escaped the cannonading of yesterday. there are thousands of Soldiers in the town and Nothing escapes their ravages. pianos, marble stands, Settees, beds are broken. Some with Shots bursting in the house and others by the Soldiers. Today i saw the first Slain in battle. there is 5 dead rebs lying where they were Shot by our Men while laying the pontoon bridge yesterday. one had his head entirely off. it was a horrid Sight for the first one. the day is clear and moderately warm. we lay concealed from the rebs by a bank although this afternoon they get our range and shell us severe for a short time, wounding 3 in our Reg and Killing two in another. our batteries Silence them in about 10 Minutes. we lay on our arms all night in front of the enemy without any molestation.

Dec 13th. This Morning we Move to the centre of the line and lie there until 4ock when we Move on the left wing but get in no part of the fight. the ball opened at 9 ock. After driving the pickets in, the batteries kept up the fire all day long very brisk on the left wing. at 2 ock the right wing became engaged and continued through the afternoon. we lie on the field again tonight.

Dec 14 (Sunday). this Morning we March back to the citty. the firing commenced on both wings by daylight, mostly musketry, but lasts but an hour and no firing the rest of the day. we lay in town all day.

Decem 15th. This Morning finds us still in the citty. through the Night Siege Guns have been planted on the hill commanding the Reb Batteries. they are not used today, however, and we lay here all day until dusk when we silently recross the river. March 2 ½ Miles to our old camp ground…."

In later notes, probably made in 1867, Rhodes returned to his memories of Fredericksburg, commenting on the lethal effectiveness of Rebel sharpshooters firing from cellars and buildings in the city, the impact of Union cannon fire on buildings, and on the shameful behavior of soldiers —including himself —in conflict. Rhodes confesses:

"As an instance of how a spirit of destruction will possess one among such havoc, I entered one of the fine brick residence[s] other soldiers were already in. One was playing a very fine piano, standing in the parlor. Another soldier struck one of the legs of the instrument with an ax knocking it completely off. The player (soldier) was a fine one and resented this injury of a fine instrument. The other said it had accompanyed Rebel songs and that was enough. Going into an adjoining parlor, I saw a beautiful French clock standing on the mantel and ticking away as though the folks had not deserted it, or two or three shells wrought havock in other portions of the house. I stepped up to it, broke the glass shield covering it, tore off the dial, ran my fingers into the wheels and lifting it from the shelf gave it a side snap, and it was a wreck and would not measure Rebel time any more. I was ashamed of myself in a minute and wished I might restore it. The move was entirely foreign to my nature. I never repeated the act again."

January 24, 1863 we moved up the River to a position opposite Falmouth where General Hooker, now in command, proposed to cross his army, Burnside having failed to force the enemy at Fredericksburg. February 11 we break camp at Falmouth, took cars to Acquia Creek where we transfer to the transport "John Brooks" to go down the Potomac. At 12 o'clock we enter Chesapeake Bay. Morning of the 13th after reporting to General Dix commanding Fortress Monroe, we start up the James River. An eight miles' run from Fortress Monroe brings us to our landing and new camp. The whole 9th Corps was sent here to recruit in health. We being in that Corps is how we (fresh troops) come to be here. It proves to be a most delightful camp.[41]

---

41   Falmouth is across the Rapahannock from Fredericksburg. Fortress Monroe guarded the entrance to Hampton Roads, at the mouth of the James and Elizabeth Rivers. The commander at Fortress Monroe, General John Adams Dix (1798-1879) was a "political" general, having served as U.S. Senator from New York and as Secretary of the Treasury prior to the war; Dix played an important role in preventing Maryland's secession in 1861 through the simple expedient of arresting the Maryland legislature. At the time when the 27th New Jersey reported, Dix was commanding general of the District of Virginia.

It is at times difficult to know how to read Rhodes— whether he is serious or is engaging in a soldier's dark sarcasm. For example, on January 6, 1863, three weeks after the bloody, senseless slaughter of the Union forces at Fredericksburg, Rhodes wrote:

> "today it rains with a cold wind. the whole Ninth Army Corps was reviewed by General Burnside in person. as he rode by cheer after cheer went up— thousands of Brave and patriotic hearts. although he was unsuccessful in his effort to drive the enemy, all honor to him who would have led us to victory but for the Simple thing of the Pontoons not being on hand in time. May he live to crown his head with Victory as he well deserves."

Similarly, we have Rhodes's description of the North Newport News campsite, which in his contemporaneous diary he describes as being "the Most pleasant Ground for camping" the regiment had ever had, even though a few days before he observed:

On February 19, 1863, we draw A tents and abandon the shelter or dog tents that we have used throughout our whole winter campaign. The shelter tent is made of common sheeting. Each man carries two pieces about six feet square each. Buttons on two sides and button holes on the other two sides. The two pieces are buttoned together and a ridge pole, usually a musket, supported at the end makes a tent for two men. It may be slept in either way— lengthwise or crosswise. If the ends are closed, a similar piece buttoned on at each end closes the tent. Any number of pieces may be buttoned together making a tent of any desired length. Usually four bunked together. We often had to clean away deep snow, pitch this little muslin tent, and make ourselves *comfortable*. There could be no fire in them unless they were stockaded, which was usually done in permanent camps and where timber could be had. In that case we built up logs—log cabin-style—one to four feet high and used our tents as a roof covering. February 23rd ground frozen hard, ice half inch thick. We remained here until March 19 when we drew five days rations and marched to Newport News Landing in a severe snow storm and waiting until March 21 when we went aboard the transport, steamed down the James to the Bay, up the Chesapeake Bay and on the morning of the 23rd reached Baltimore and took

---

"the Ground covered with Snow. At 7 ock it commences raining, the watter[sic] running through our tents and over the bottom. the Ground to[o] level for ditching. watter enough in tent for washing, which i do. the wind blowing almost a gale. it continues raining all day. Everything wet and uncomfortable. the regimental Guards are dispensed with, also the pickets."

cars for Parkersburg, Ohio, via the Baltimore and Ohio Railroad. On the morning of March 25th we go aboard the transport and on the following morning, the 26th, we start down the River for Cincinnati, which was reached early on the 27th.

By 2 P.M. we leave Covington, Kentucky, by rail for Lexington, which we reach about midnight. In the morning of the 28th we run to Nicholasville, Ky. From here we marched. We were in the Johnnies' country sure, and some part of our column had a brush with them every few hours. It seemed to be a strong force of raiders foraging for supplies for the Southern Army. We go in camp March 29, for a few days a half mile from Camp Dick Robinson.[42] Our camp is on the Widow Dunn's place and her house is Brigade Headquarters. There are plenty of Rebel prisoners marching north. They are a motley lot, their clothes like Jacob's coat of many colors.

April 11th we quit camp. At dusk of that day we reach Stafford [ed: Stanford] and camp one and one-half miles beyond, making twenty miles that day with heavy knapsacks and very warm and dusty. At 2 P.M. April 25, we broke camp and took the road again with two day's rations in haversack and ten days in Brigade wagons. April 26 we made 23 mile on foot and very warm. On the 28th we reached the Cumberland River at Simpson's Ford—too high, could not cross—and

---

42   Nicholasville, Kentucky, 12 miles south of Lexington, was the terminus of the Covington and Lexington Railway and thus the railhead for Union operations. Camp Dick Robinson, another 12 miles further south on what is now U.S. Route 27 near the tiny cross-roads of Bryantsville, had been a key assembly point and base of Kentucky's pro-Union forces in 1861.

marched back to Somerset and took another road. April 30 we reach the River by 8 A.M. and cross on pontoon boats, river flat boats. May 1st after skirmishing with the enemy all day, we reach the town of Monticello, Ky., in the afternoon.[43] Our regiment is detached here from the remainder of the Corps, our time of enlistment having about expired. May 5, we break camp at Monticello and start toward home. On the following day at 8 A.M. we again reached the Cumberland River, which was raging from recent rains. One of the pontoons containing about sixty of our regiment capsized in the middle of the stream. One Captain, one Sergeant and thirty-one privates were drowned in plain sight of us all and not fifty yards away, and they were all homeward bound. We go into a very pleasant comfortable camp at Somerset and remain there until June 4.[44] On June 7 we reach

---

43   The campaign took them progressively south, roughly down what is now U.S. Route 27, toward the Tennessee border. Stanford is about 20 miles south of Camp Dick Robinson, by way of Lancaster; Somerset is another 33 miles south, just a few miles north of the Cumberland River; and, as a crow flies, Monticello, Kentucky is roughly 25 miles southwest of Somerset. As Rhodes's daily diary from the campaign suggests, this was a rather more difficult march than his laconic re-telling might indicate, and without the benefit of foreknowledge or hindsight, rather more stressful. Though it remained in the Union, Kentucky had considerable secessionist sympathies, and the Union force of which Rhodes's regiment was a part was trying to repel an elusive Confederate body that repeatedly threatened but eluded battle— though even this clarity was lacking at the time. Again, it is difficult to judge with certainty whether Rhodes was being deliberately ironic when he wrote, on May 5 as his regiment was about to begin to retrace its steps: "our whole force is on the retreat, having Succeeded in driving the rebs acrost the Tennessee line."

44   As the year progressed, Rhodes's contemporaneous notes bore increasing indication of a sense of the huge waste and tragedy of the war, though still recording appropriate patriotic fervor. As the end of the nine-month enlistment loomed closer, the desire to return to home and to civilian life became ever more

apparent. The senselessness of the tragedy of May 6, as the regiment was finally apparently "out of the war" seems to have brought these sentiments and musings into clearer focus for Rhodes. Though here in his autobiography Rhodes moves on from the event without even a new paragraph, in his contemporaneous writing the event yields a clearer shift in tone.

> "Tonight ours is a Sad regt. the Shock everyone feels. So Sudden was it and So heartrending, bringing Sorrow to Many in the regt to Say Nothing of those at home who are anxiously awaiting their return, which but for this woud ere long had the pleasure, but alas, for those few they were Not permitted to enjoy it but found a watery grave beneath the turbid waters of the Cumberland."

Rhodes's sarcasm becomes a bit more certain from this point on —for example, his observation on May 18 that

> "Today Gen. Carter received a Note under flag of truce from the rebs who hold again the opposite Side of the river, wishing to exchange a prisoner for a Sack of Salt, but Gen. Carter Could Not See it. perhaps they [ed.: presumably General Carter] think they [ed.: presumably the "rebs"] will Spoil this hot weather. No drill. Dress parade ends the duties the day."

It is of course dangerous to try to read too much into brief diary entries, but it is possible to see an increasing sense of common identity with the ordinary soldiers on the other side and increasing sense of separation from the authorities—political and military—directing the war. On May 29 for example:

> "the rebel pickets continue on the opposite Side of the river…. they hitch their horses in the Orchard upon the bank and come to the waters edge to wash and lounge. they Seem Strongly to desire our pickets to hold conversation with them, but the orders from Headquarters interdicting it Stand in the way and with the exception of a word Now and then little is Said on either Side. the River is So low as to be easily forded by infantry at this and other ferries in Kentucky."

From this point on, Rhodes also speaks more frequently of deaths and burials, and of impatience to be out of the war. On June 1:

> "Nine months this Morning we left our homes for the Seat of war, and all expected their time out at this time. by an order from the War Department, we are to Stay until the 19th of the present Month, causing No little disappointment with officers and Men. the day clear and warm. we buried another of our comrades in arms today. he died yesterday very Sudden and in his tent with No One with him at the time of his death. he was an old Man."

the Kentucky River and cross at Hickman's Bridge and camp in a beautiful grove on land owned by Mr. John Hanley, a very wealthy planter and a large slave owner.[45] We are here until June 16. Then on through Cincinnati and Columbus to Wheeling, West Virginia, which we reach on the 18th. On June 19th we attended the inaugural ceremonies of the new state of West Virginia. On Sunday, the 21st, we were sent from Wheeling to Uniontown, to repel an anticipated raid into the place, and went into camp on the Fair Grounds. We finally reached Newark, N.J., and were mustered out of the service on September 3, 1863.

---

45   Hickman Bridge was a key crossing point on the Kentucky River between Nicholasville and Camp Dick Robinson. A large Army base, Camp Nelson, had been constructed here to guard the bridge and to serve as a depot for operations in Kentucky. The comment regarding Hanley and his land was consistent with Rhodes's careful eye for the economics of the countryside, villages, and towns through which he passed. Especially as his personal involvement in the war wound down, Rhodes became an increasingly observant student of agricultural conditions and commerce. But more than anything else, Rhodes was interested in how technology and economics intersected. His entry for June 7 —in which he muses on John Hanley, a presumably loyal planter who happened to have three sons and several grandsons in the Rebel Army— is the longest in his diary. Despite his rural background and lack of exposure to anything more modern or large-scale than a small-town tinsmith's hardware store, Rhodes seems to begin to grasp the future not only of warfare but of the American economy. In part he muses:

> "it [Camp Robinson] is at present the Headquarters of the Army of Kentucky and preparations on a large Scale are going on. large Bakeries, extensive hospital Buildings as well as all kinds of Manufacturing Shops for army purposes are going up. a Railroad Soon to be commenced, running from here to Nicholasville, is calling an army of Mechanics and laborers, who find ready employment and good wages. it is to be built by the Govt. Thousands of Dollars have been lost or Might have been Saved had there been R.R. communication with this place. in fact it is impossible to invade Tennessee Successfully from this point without it, as Supplies are So long getting up owing to the distance transported by teams."

[sic: July 3, 1863] We reached Deckertown again a few days later, well and sound, not having been wounded nor sick, except for a couple of weeks at Emery Hospital with a bad case of mumps.[46]

Nelson Stoddard was in the same Company as myself and we shared the same tent during the time we were in the service. John Howell and House mostly tented with us when in one camp for a time.[47]

My situation at Overhiser's was open to me on my return. Also Hornbeck and Beemer, the leading mercantile firm of Deckertown, wished me to take a rival shop and store they had started in the place, offering to let me have it cheap and pay as I could. This was a good opportunity to go

---

46   Interestingly, in his contemporaneous diary, Rhodes is silent as to the nature of the illness that briefly sidelined him in Washington, near the start of the war. Writing later—when he was between 61 and 72 years of age—Rhodes is able to name the disease, and in doing so hint at the disease's probable consequences—sterility. As a consequence of the war, whatever mark Rhodes was going to make on the world would come in some form other than parenthood.

47   In his contemporaneous diary of his nine months of service, Rhodes mentions by name any of his fellow soldiers only four times—once to identify the first soldier of his company to die, once to name a soldier who was the second of three brothers to die, once to name the five men with whom he typically tented, and a second time to name them again and to mention two soldiers returned from the hospital. Two observations seem worth underscoring. The first is that whatever personal ties Rhodes may have forged with the men who soldiered alongside of him, these did not seem significant enough to him to merit any mention even at the time. His later self-appraisal that he was something of a "loner" seems entirely consistent with his contemporaneous reporting. This noted, it is also of interest whom his tent-mates were: his "best friend" (who goes unmentioned except on the two occasions when tent-mates were identified) First Sergeant Nelson Stoddard; Sergeant John C. Howell (1842–1895); Sergeant Peter A. House (1835–1889); Corporal Lemuel F. Sutton (1833–1897); and Sergeant John Fountain. He was, in other words, typically tenting with four of the five sergeants (that is, senior non-commissioned officers) in the company. Loner or not, socially he was part of the company's leadership cadre.

into business where I was acquainted and with a prospect of establishing myself. Wishing to visit some, I did not decide then. I had both the need and desire to take a course in some commercial school before settling down to business again. In fact I could not now rid myself for the desire for a better education, although I had an average common school education for that time, but I expected to be in business for myself and would need it to more nearly even up in the struggle.

I visited relatives and friends in New Jersey, then went to Aurora, New York, to see Mr. Winch and acquaintances there. There I met Mr. Warren Higley, Principal of the old Cayuga Lake Academy, an old and very prominent boys' and girls' boarding and day school.[48] I had never met Mr. Higley, but knew all about the school. For more than three years I had known every boy and girl student and envied them their opportunities. The Academy would not open yet for several weeks. Meeting Mr. Higley one day, I told him how I was situated and what I wished to do. He was self-made, very earnest, sympathetic, and at once participated in my desire and urged me to enter the Academy. It was such an opportunity as I had wished for but more elaborate, not so commercial, as I had thought of taking. I had several talks with him. He

---

48   The Cayuga Lake Academy was founded in 1797. Warren Higley (born 1833), was raised on a farm in the Finger Lakes region of New York State, graduated from Hamilton College in 1862, and served as principal of the Cayuga Lake Academy from 1863 to 1868. Thus Higley, only five years Rhodes's senior, would have just assumed his duties at Cayuga Lake Academy when Rhodes met him. While his career path moved in a different direction, Higley—like Rhodes—offers an interesting case study of social mobility, the accumulation of human capital, and the emergence of a national, professional class. After his stint as principal of the academy, Higley went on to study law and served as a judge in Cincinnati before moving his legal practice to New York City.

made it seem so easy and natural for me to enter the school that I about made up my mind to do so for one year only.... [Ellipsis in original.]

I continued my visit on to Millport, Pine Valley (the old home), and Troy, Pennsylvania. Returning from Troy, I had to change cars at Elmira and then and there on the depot platform had to decide whether I would take the Erie train back to Deckertown and engage in business, or the Canandagua train for Aurora and school. The latter train came first to the platform and I took it. It proved to be a turning point in my life—one of those events that many attribute to chance or a "happen-so." Not so. I believe it was direction which I did not see. I believe all the events of our lives, that give important direction or fundamentally affect them, are directed by Him who moves in mysterious ways in His dealings with us. Nonetheless a Mystery or direction because done through natural agencies.

I entered the Cayuga Lake Academy at Aurora, New York, at the fall term in September, 1863. Boarded and roomed in the building—southwest corner room on the fourth floor. Had that room during the whole time I was at the Academy. It was a pleasant, but very trying year for me, especially at our Friday rhetoricals. All the scholars belonged to one of two Societies and each Society was represented before the assembled school and visiting strangers every Friday afternoon. There was declamation, composition, and recitation. The Principal, Mr. Higley, was no respecter of persons in making assignments for these exercises. The poorest declaimers came first, the best, last. The same was true for composition. I had had no practice in either, could not compete in inflection, gesture, and stage form with a number of the boys twelve or fourteen years old and was called upon before they were. I was then 24 years old, the oldest in the school. I knew all the scholars, most of them young men and women. I also knew all the visitors, for I had been in the store and shop in Aurora over three years. It was a most trying ordeal to be classed below such small boys in these public exercises. After one or two trials I went to Mr. Higley, and with determination told him that I must be excused from declamation or I must quit the school. I could not bear the mortification. He had been a farmer boy before he went to Union College [sic: Hamilton College] and knew how it was for himself. I remained, but resolved I would soon be the best. Generally the boys selected their pieces from rhetorical books. I was full of the war spirit and commenced condensing from some of the patriotic speeches, Henry Ward Beecher's oration on Raising the Flag over Sumter and such like.[49] These I could feel, and their recital thrilled me. I could lose my individuality in the fervor of my theme. I made the halls resound and the woods reecho with my practice. In a very short time I had a place among three or four of the best declaimers in the school, but I had passed through a veritable furnace. At the close of the academic year, July 21, 1864, five of the best speakers in a school where speaking was specialized, were selected for orations. I was called third. Albert J. Leffingwell and Charles K. Hoyt, the two who came after me, were young men far advanced in studies. The other two were first Reuben T. Stiles, the

---

49   Presumably Rhodes was thinking of other patriotic speeches. Beecher's "Raising the Flag" speech was delivered only in mid-April 1865, midway through Rhodes's final term.

second, R.T. Griggs.[50] At the close of the fall term the following year, March 23, 1865, I had the last speech, and at the close of the spring term, July 21, 1865, I had the final oration and valedictory. I do not write this as laudatory, simply as something accomplished.

At the close of my first academic year, I was more anxious to continue another year than I ever was to commence; remained with Mr. Winch during the summer and in September took my old room at the Academy for another school year. Was graduated the following July.

I was now prepared to enter a scientific course in college. Mr. Higley strongly advised that I do so. I had pursued studies that led directly into college for their completion. But going to college, though immediately in sight and more than inviting to me, was beyond my means. I commenced at the Academy with but $200.00 and upon leaving, was in debt $50.00 to Mr. Higley for board and room. He never charged me anything for tuition. We had often talked

---

50   To understand the social and educational processes at work, it is worth taking a quick look at life trajectories of the four classmates that Rhodes identifies. Albert Tracy Leffingwell (1845–1916) was the son and grandson of medical doctors; after graduating from Cayuga Lake Academy he enrolled at Hamilton College but dropped out to begin medical studies in New York City. After graduation he continued his studies in London, Paris, and Vienna, and became a noted American psychologist and author, writing *inter alia* on vivisection, suicide, free will, free trade, and his travels in Japan. He also traveled extensively in Europe, in North Africa and the Middle East, and in East, Southeast, and South Asia. Charles K. Hoyt (born about 1846) graduated from Hamilton College, was ordained, served as principal of the Cayuga Lake Academy, and became the professor of Rhetoric and English Language at newly created Wells College. Reuben T. Stiles (1842–1905) was, like Rhodes, a veteran of the Civil War; he graduated from Kalamazoo College in 1870 but appears to have pursued a career in farming. Rufus Theron Griggs (1845–c.1929), who seems to have come from a prosperous and progressive Aurora-area family, went on to graduate from Hamilton College in 1869, and then, after a brief stint as a teacher, to pursue a long legal career in Brooklyn.

about my future course, and he knew I had not a dollar to do with. At the close of school he surprised me by offering to let me have what money I would require to complete a college course. Four boys that graduated with me would go on to college that fall. I was greatly surprised and felt complimented by his generous offer. Of course, I would repay it. He was a comparatively young man of limited means. The more I thought of the matter, the more I felt that I could not conscientiously accept it, for if something should happen to me, he could not afford to lose the money, and I finally told him so. He would not give up and without my knowledge spoke to Honorable E.B. Morgan, a wealthy gentleman of the place whom I had known for five or six years and who knew me as well. Mr. Morgan asked me to come down to his house one evening in the forepart of September, '65. I went; he took me into his library and said: "Daniel, what are you going to do now?" I replied that I should like to take a course in college but that was out of the question, and I expected to go into a store until I could do better. He replied, "I will furnish you means to complete your course of study." I asked, "How can I secure you? Get my life insured in your favor?" He replied, "Daniel, I have known you intimately for a number of years, under different conditions. If you live and keep your health, I will get my money; if not, it will be the worse for yourself." Thereupon he wrote me a check for $100.00. The next day I started for Michigan University at Ann Arbor, Michigan. I entered the Freshman Class of '69, and graduated with it as Civil Engineer.[51]

---

51   Edwin Barber Morgan (1806–1881) grew up in a local merchant family and pursued a career as a highly successful capitalist. A business associate of Henry Wells, Morgan served as the first president of Wells Fargo

Whenever I needed funds during the four years, I wrote him and received a check promptly, and I as promptly sent him my note.

I was through college, what next? I was in my 30th year, had a theoretical, but no practical knowledge of my profession—and $1400.00 in debt. Nine years before, I left Mr. Winch better equipped practically than I was at this time and no debt. But how much the six years of study and association had widened my mental horizon and increased my capacity for self-enjoyment and influence to others! If we live in thought and feeling rather than figures on a dial, how much larger my life. Money or its equivalent we must have, but money is only a means. The other is its own reward.

My University life was very pleasant. The work was hard, but I could keep up with it. I was at some disadvantage for lack of longer preparatory study. One commencing at school when young and continuing his studies until he is prepared for college has a great advantage there, and other things being near equal, will do his work easier and make more progress than one like myself leaving district school for several years of business life, then taking a two year's preparatory course. I passed entrance examinations

---

and a director of American Express; he was also an original shareholder in *The New York Times*. In addition to banking and shipping concerns, Morgan was involved in a wide range of other entrepreneurial activities, including railroads, shipbuilding, starch production, and gypsum mining. Morgan served in the U.S. House of Representatives from 1853 to 1859, was on the board of Cornell University, and was a founder of Wells College, as well as being a supporter of the Cayuga Lake Academy. The "house" to which Rhodes was invited would have been Morgan's mansion at 431 Main Street, Aurora, built in 1857–1858 for the sum of $50,000; the mansion, now the property of Wells College, was in 1980 added to the National Register of Historic Places.

and passed all (except twice) during the University course. I had to live economically, and with hundreds of others boarded mostly at student clubs. For part of one year three of us (Lester McLean and Hugh Alexander) roomed together and boarded ourselves at Watt's Jewelry Store. Mr. A.A. Robinson was the third one before I came in.[52] I bought his right and title to all and sundry. The record

---

52   If the Civil War were an important growing experience and prompt for seeking a professional career, and if academies like the one at Cayuga Lake offered a route for acquiring the necessary foundation, then the University of Michigan was clearly a critical generator of professional human capital. Because they offer illustrations not unlike Rhodes's own, it is useful to look at his roommates.

Lester McLean (1846–1904) came from a modest background—his father was a Methodist preacher in rural Pennsylvania and Ohio. Although he was studying literature, he worked his way through college with summer employment on the Great Lakes Survey (as Rhodes also may have done) and took time off to work as a teacher to earn the money necessary for continued enrollment. McLean was class president of the graduating class of 1872. Going on to receive his law degree—which he paid for by working as a high school principal —he practiced law in Ohio before moving west and eventually establishing his legal practice in Denver. Hugh Byron Alexander (1847–1930) of Geneva, Illinois, pursued an engineering career, working under classmate A.A. Robinson (and with Rhodes) on the Atchison, Topeka, and Santa Fe in the 1880s, and ultimately pursuing a career with the Chicago Sanitation Commission. Alexander came from an even more modest background than McLean, being the son of a blacksmith.

The most interesting and important of the classmates was Robinson, with whom Rhodes roomed in his senior year. Like Rhodes, Albert Alonzo Robinson (born 1844) pursued a railroad career, largely with the Atchison, Topeka, and Santa Fe road, where he played a critical role in the road's extraordinary success and growth. It was Robinson who facilitated Rhodes's move to the west, and it was Robinson who appointed Rhodes to increasingly senior positions with that company. Ultimately, when not named president of the company, Robinson left the Santa Fe to become President of the Mexican Central Railroad. Like his roommates, Robinson came from a modest background: his father, who died when Robinson was five, was a Vermont farmer. He and his brothers, however, attended college, the oldest becoming an inventor and professor of mechanical engineering.

stands: "Feb. 9, 1867, Commenced rooming at Watt's. Paid Robinson $10.00 for his proportion of room rent until June 20th and $4.00 for his share or interest in the furniture on hand and assumed his account and pledged myself to continue the same as before. The account this day stands: Alexander paid in $42.00; McLain [sic], $36.09; Robinson, $41.80."

The latter amount I assumed. Each kept account of what he paid out. The others did the cooking. I bought.

Record: Feb. 13, loaf bread, 10¢;
14th, 2 ¼ # butter @ 30¢, 72¢;
16th, 2 loaves, 20¢, ginger, 10¢;
17th, milk tickets, $1.00;
18th, loaf bread, 10¢;
19th, bread, 10¢, 2 ¼ lb. butter @33¢, 88¢; 5 lb sugar @16¢, 80¢;
23rd, 2 loaves bread, 20¢, 1 bottle lemon extract, 20¢;
24th, bread, 10¢;
26th, 2 loaves bread and cheese, 60¢;
29th, bread, 10¢;
March 1st, bread, 10¢;
3rd, bread, 10¢;
6th, bread and crackers, 40¢, for wood sawed, $1.50;
7th, bread and soda, 40¢;
9th, bread, 10¢;
11th, cinnamon and cheese, 55¢;
12th, bread, 10¢;
13th, buns, 17¢;
14th, buns, 10¢;
15th, bread, 10¢;
16th, bread and cake, 50¢;
19th, bread, 10¢;

20th, cheese, 32¢;

21st, kerosene, 30¢;

25th, 2 breads and vinegar, 30¢;

26th, apples and 2 breads, 40¢;

27th, 5 lb. sugar @ 14c, 70¢; 2 breads and herring, 32¢;

29th, 2 lb 10 oz. butter, 85¢;

30th, load wood, $4.50, 2 breads, 20¢;

April 1st, for sawing wood, $1.25, bread, 10¢;

4th, meat, 18¢; 5th, butter, 83¢, bread, 10¢, cheese, 40¢;

6th, flour, $2.05, 2 breads, 20¢, buns, 12¢;

9th, bread, 10¢;

10th, bread and ½ doz. eggs, 19¢;

13th, bread and buns, 16¢;

14th, bread and ½ doz. eggs, 20¢;

15th, kerosene, 30¢;

16th, bread, 10¢;

22nd, bread, and eggs, 29¢;

23rd, bread, 10¢;

26th, bread and nutmegs, 15¢;

27th, bread and cake, 18¢;

29th, bread, 10¢; 30th, bread and cake, 18¢;

May 2nd, bread and cake, 18¢;

3rd, milk tickets, 50¢;

4th, matches and bread, 30c, chocolate, 25¢, eggs, 14¢;

6th, bread, 10¢, wood, $1.60;

7th, bread, 10¢, cakes, 25¢;

8th, butter and lettuce, 71¢;

9th, eggs, 30¢;

13th, 2 bread, 20¢;

14th, 2 lb. butter, 56¢, 2 breads, 20¢;

20th, 2 breads and cake, 28¢;

22nd, pineapple, 30¢;
24th, bread and eggs, 40¢;
31st, eggs and beans, 58¢, bread, 10¢;
June 3rd, bread, 10¢; 5th, cake, 16¢.

Total to June 5th, Rhodes, $72.28; McLean, $72.60; Alexander, $70.84. For three persons, room and board during college year, September to June, $215.78. Average for each, $71.92.

This is the first and last time I ever boarded myself. Did not like it.[53] One year my roommate was George B. Lake[54] and the last year, A.A. Robinson.

I received from Hon. E.B. Morgan as follows:

Sept. 15, 1865, $100.00;
June 20, 1866, $75.00;
April 18, 1866, $50.00;
October 19, 1866, $100.00;
January 18, 1867, $50.00;
March 23, 1867, $50.00;
May 25, 1867, $35.00;
October 11, 1867, $100.00;
January 25, 1868, $50.00;
April 11, 1868, $50.00;

---

53   If Rhodes and his roommates actually lived on this diet, it is hardly surprising that he "did not like it." More surprising perhaps, or at least more revealing, is that Rhodes kept this careful account book for another 30 or more years, despite having no fixed abode and pursuing a career of constant travel.

54   George B. Lake (1845–1884) was another civil engineering classmate who pursued a career with the Atchison, Topeka, and Santa Fe road, reaching the position of the railroad's chief engineer – a position previously occupied by Robinson and in which he was succeeded by Rhodes. Lake was the son of a some-time teacher, some-time farmer in central Michigan.

June 4, 1868, $40.00;
October 29, 1868, $100.00;
March 12, 1869, $100.00.

Total exclusive of interest, $900.00. With interest and exchange, $1286.00.

When I graduated from the University June, 1869, at the age of 32, I was in debt $1400.00, without assets except education and experience.

May 1, 1869 I received the appointment as Assistant in the United States Lake Survey, a branch of the United States Coast Survey, and left Detroit May 4, as Assistant to the Chief of Survey and Astronomical Party, Mr. O.B. Wheeler of Detroit, an old Government civil employee, graduate of the University of Michigan.[55] We took the U.S. Steamer "Search" and went directly to Michipocoten Island in Lake Superior, landed and made camp.[56] There were two [other] similar parties on the boat. They were landed at different points on the north shore of the Lake in Canada. Our work was primary triangulation and latitude and longitude work. The three parties work in connection, one at the

---

55   O.B. Wheeler (died 1896) received his A.B. from Michigan in 1862 and an AM and MS in 1865; in 1879 he was awarded an honorary degree. While tasked with mapping, these survey parties were in effect wide-ranging scientific missions, returning with geological and botanical samples and providing the material for a clear assessment of the economic potential of the wilderness territory they were surveying. There is some evidence that Rhodes may also have worked the prior summer for Wheeler and the United States Lake Survey: the University of Michigan herbarium reported specimens in its holdings collected by Wheeler, "D.H. Rhoads," and others on Isle Royale in 1868.

56   Michipocoten or Michipicoten Island is a large, uninhabited island in the Canadian portion of Lake Superior.

apex of great triangles, the sides of which were from 30 to 90 miles long, and the parties were separated by that distance. We being the pivotal party remained at our station until the close of work in the fall. The other parties changed location from time to time around the north shore, but we were always on one apex of their triangles. Each party measured the angle between the other two parties. The mean of several hundred transit readings taken on different days and by the Chief and Assistant determined the angle within a probable error of a very few seconds of arc.

We had a fine astronomical instrument and every night that it was clear observed for latitude and longitude, and made night communication with the other parties by powder flashes, that is, each party determined its own local time by its observations. About midnight a series of flashes would be made by each, and each would note by the chronometer to the fraction of a second the time of the flash. The light being instantaneous, the difference in the recorded time of each party would be the difference in time between two places, and time is longitude. In this way longitude was established beyond telegraphic points, and as these were made at the apex of each great triangle, the longitude and latitude of each point was determined astronomically and could be definitely located upon the Earth's surface.

One side of our triangles was from our Island to Kewenau Point, a distance of 90 miles over Lake Superior. The actual lines of vision ran through the water eight miles on account of the curvature of the Earth, and we would see the mirror reflections or heliotrope light only when reflection was excessive. Michipocoten Island is about seven by nine miles, mountainous and wooded. There was but one family on it when we were there. They supplied wood for the Steamer "Collingwood." As we were never at the landing, we saw no white people while there except once.

The whole Island was thickly wooded, abounded in small lakes, precipitous rocky palisades with deep wooded ravines between. From the observatory, the highest point on the Island, we could see where the landing was three or four miles distant on an air line, but not the landing itself. A point might seem but half a mile away, to reach it one might have to travel two or three miles around cliffs, lakes, and marsh. The man at the landing who once visited our shore camp, told us that there was a very fine specimen of agate in the cliffs near his place, that could be secured by a little blasting. I was determined to get some. So, during midsummer and at a time when the atmosphere was so dense from forest fires that we could not work, I one morning left the observatory camp for the landing and was to be back in a day or two. I took only a quantity of powder and a dinner lunch. For three-fourths of a mile I followed a familiar trail to where it crossed another said to lead to the landing. The landing trail had been blazed years before by hacking an occasional tree and was very difficult to follow. I followed it for about three hours, then it failed. I marked the last tree by breaking limbs and hunted for an hour in every direction for the next marked tree but found none. It was now two o'clock in the afternoon. It had rained and my clothes were wet through. I ate my lunch and debated whether I should return or go ahead. I did not want to acknowledge I could not find the landing and concluded to go ahead. I took the direction as well as I could and started, keeping it by ranging trees ahead. In a little while I struck a lake. It was bordered by willows and marsh, and I could not tell which was the shorter distance to pass it. I judged I was nearer the end to my right. After going through willows, water, and mud for some distance, I came to a point where I could see the whole lake and saw that the shortest distance around it was to my left. I took that direction and after a time passed the lake, fording a deep outlet. About this time I caught the direction of the sun and found my course was all right to strike the lake shore at the nearest point if not the landing exactly. It was by this time about sundown. I continued going until it became so dark in the woods and brush I could not pick my way. Finding a tree that had been blown up by the roots, I concluded to take what shelter it offered and get some rest and sleep. My matches were wet and I could not start a fire. My clothes were wet; I was very tired and hungry after my hard afternoon experience.

After an hour or so I became so cold I could not remain there if I had dared to, as I feared serious consequences and knew no one would ever find me if I did not get out myself. I could now hear the low roar of the surf and taking that for my direction I started again. It was so dark I could not get along very fast but kept going as that kept me warm. I crossed some small streams, some wet marshy places and some abrupt rocks, but fortunately nothing I could not get over. Late in the evening the moon came out and nearly full. From my night observations I knew my directions from it and found I did not need to change my general course. While it was dark under the thick foliage, still the moonlight helped me to get along.

About 1:00 A.M. I came to an abrupt range of rocks about fifty feet high and too steep for me to scale. I followed along the base some distance when I came to a tree that I could climb and from a limb could reach a bench in the cliff. I had no idea how far I might have to go to get around the rocks nor what I might meet with in trying to do so, and concluded to climb. With much difficulty I reached the shelf, but found it far from the top of the cliff, which seemed to loom up the higher as I went up. It was not so steep from where I landed and by slow and very cautious work I finally reached the top. I was an hour getting over, getting perhaps 300 feet horizontal. From the top I could hear the roar of the surf very plainly and knew the Lake shore could not be far away.

I could see nothing, the timber was so thick. Encouraged by the sounds from the shore and the ground not being very rough, I got along quite well. Once I came within one step of falling over a ledge twenty feet down. At 3:30 A.M. I reached the Lake shore. I was by this time so exhausted for want of sleep and some rest I had to stop. Everything was wet. I found a fallen tree. Fixing myself in the branches, I dropped to sleep at once. In less than a half hour I awoke so chilled and stiff I was alarmed. I had reached the Lake shore all right. Now the question was, Should I go to the right or to the left to find the landing? I concluded that it was to my left and started that way, believing that it could not be very far away. The walking was so bad in the edge of the woods that I took the beach and frequently had to wade in water to my knees and occasionally take to the woods to get around a deep place. I continued in this way until daylight, when I again stopped to consider what was best to do. I could not recognize the headlands nor could I see but a short distance forward or backward. Near me stood a very large and tall pine tree. It towered above the surrounding trees and in my extremity I determined to climb it and see if I could catch a glimpse of the landing. How I got nearly to the top of that tree is more and more of a mystery to me. I could not have done it before nor since. It did me no good. Our own shore camp was to my right. I was reaching the limit of my endurance. If the landing was to my right, I would not reach it going as I was. I felt I could take no chances and faced for camp, by the windings of the shore, about twelve miles distant. I had a beautiful day but what a journey for me in my condition. How did I ever make it! But I did at 1:00 A.M. the following morning. Forty-four hours with but a small lunch, traveling two days, one whole night and half another! My clothes wet one night and most of one day, through a trackless forest. Within a stone's throw of our camp an arm of the Lake ran in to a cliff. When the wind was off shore, there was little water in it. When toward shore, the water would be eight to ten feet deep. When I reached it, it was full, and I had, as a final act, to swim one hundred fifty feet, which brought me into camp dripping at 1:00 A.M. I awakened the cook and had a hot meal, a hot bath and dry clothes in short order. I was confined to the house and immediate vicinity for about two weeks. Made my own prescriptions, which were limited to what our medicine chest contained.

As the sequel proved, I kept my course so well that I struck the shore only about one mile from the Landing, which was to my left from where I struck the shore, as I at first surmised, and I would have reached it, had I gone ahead as I started.

I hardly think I would have reached home but for the numerous little streams of pure and cold water from the interior into the Lake. Often as I reached one of these, I would throw myself upon the beach, drink and bathe my face and head. This always refreshed me for a little time. I frequently had to make long detours into the woods to get around some bold headlands running out into deep water. A number of times I threw myself upon the beach and thought I could possibly go no further. And as often made another effort, knowing that it depended absolutely upon myself whether I got through or left my bones where they would never be found. I looked death in the face several times on that trip and but for my splendid physique I never would have got through.[57]

---

57   This is the only story in Rhodes's writings, including his contemporaneous Civil War diary, in which he acknowledges any fear or concern about his physical survival or well-being. This experience was clearly an extraordinarily powerful one for him. Indeed, presumably with his encouragement, one of Rhodes's nephews developed this tale into an unpublished novelette. As always, it is dangerous to read too much into an account such as this, but it is intriguing that Rhodes's adversary, potential nemesis, but also aid, is nature in its untamed

Returning in the fall, we reached Detroit October 30, 1869. On November 15, I commenced work as levelman on the survey of the Toledo and Ann Arbor Railroad, from Ann Arbor to Toledo. Completed the survey in January, 1870. During the winter made some surveys from Ann Arbor north to Owasso [sic: Owosso], Mich.[58]

On April 21, 1870, I went to Waterloo, Indiana, as Assistant Engineer to Mr. H.A. Parker, who was Division Engineer in charge of construction of the Ft. Wayne and Jackson Railroad, from Angola south. Angola was then the operating terminus. In about six weeks Mr. Parker left, and I was given his position and remained until the road was completed into Fort Wayne (October 20, 1870). A Mr. Wood was Chief Engineer.[59]

November 11, 1870, I went to Winona, Michigan, as Division Engineer on construction of the extension of the Jackson, Lansing and Saginaw R.R. north from

---

condition, and—apart from the reference to "splendid physique" which may or may not have been dark humor—victory over this adversary is represented as depending on careful observation and scientific reason.

58 A levelman was a junior member of a survey team, typically responsible for operating the survey level to help establish elevation, for keeping various notes, and for helping to supervise manual workers associated with the survey. Toledo, Ohio is about 52 miles south of Ann Arbor. Actual construction of the line appears to have been the victim of the crash of 1873, and completion of the Ann Arbor-Toledo railroad project delayed about twenty years. Owosso, Michigan lies west of Flint, Michigan, about 65 miles northwest of Ann Arbor.

59 Waterloo, Indiana is about 29 miles north of Fort Wayne, in the northeastern corner of the state. Angola, Indiana is a further 15 miles north on old Route 27. H.A. Parker was a successful railway engineer, helping to build and operate a number of railroads in the Midwest, often associated with the Rock Island railroad system, where he rose to hold senior executive positions. As Rhodes's own career is testimony, frequent reassignments and employment shifts were the norm for railroad engineering professionals.

Winona twenty-five miles.[60]   By December 19, winter
had set in so we had to suspend work. Mr. H.H. Smith,
Chief Construction Manager for James F. Joy, President
of the Michigan Central R.R., wrote me to come to
Lansing at once and take a Division from Lansing east
twenty-five miles on construction of the Detroit, Lansing
and Lake Michigan R.R., salary, $150 per month.[61]

On the following day (20th) I was at Lansing, secured
an office and was ready to commence laying out work.
My brother Will was my assistant. In the fall of 1871
the line was completed to Lansing and connection made
with the portion constructed from Lansing to Greenville,
Michigan. I was then sent to Greenville to do some
work between there and Howard, the junction with the
Grand Rapids and Indiana R.R. Afterward I surveyed
and located a branch line into Stanton, Michigan.[62]

---

60   Winona, Michigan was a tiny hamlet in Michigan's Upper Peninsula—
the portion of the state located north of Wisconsin, in the triangle of land
separating Lake Superior and Lake Michigan. Winona itself is in Elm River
Township, at the base of a small peninsula jutting out into Lake Superior. Twenty-
five miles north would have brought the railroad to Houghton, Michigan.

61   James Frederick Joy (1810–1896), educated at Dartmouth College
and Harvard Law School, was an enormously successful Detroit-based
railroad lawyer and executive, and major figure in the early Republican Party.
Joy came from a very modest background—his father was a blacksmith in
Durham, NH. He worked his way through law school, taking time off as a
teacher at an academy and as a tutor at Dartmouth, to finance his studies.
From the writing of the Michigan Central's original private charter in 1846
until near his death 50 years later, Joy masterminded the construction and
operation of a number of the upper midwest's major railroads and their
expansion into the Great Plains. He served in the Michigan Legislature
during the Civil War and as a regent of the University of Michigan.

62   Greenville, Michigan lies roughly 50 miles northwest of Lansing.
Howard City is a further 21 miles to the northwest. Stanton is 12 miles
northeast from Greenville.

On January 8, 1872 Mr. H.H. Smith wired me to report at once for work on the Detroit and Bay City R.R. and bring my instruments. At once I went to Oxford, organized a party, and located the line south from there thirteen miles. Then went to Vassar and located south to Otter Lake, thirteen miles. Then went back to Bay City and located back to Vassar, twenty-three miles. It was now spring and time for constructing. I took the Division from Otter Lake to Bay City. James P. Green, levelman, Brother Will, rodman and extra levelman. Office at Vassar.[63]

As the reference to brother Will suggests, Rhodes was now sufficiently established to begin to take on the task of looking after two of his younger brothers, Charley and Will, now aged 22 and 20, who had been drifting through New York state and Pennsylvania in a variety of unskilled labor positions. Will's account of how he and Charley found their way back to Rhodes is interesting. In mid-1870 the brothers were employed as the driver and the conductor of a hotel omnibus in boomtown Oil City, Pennsylvania.

"[E]arly in the fall we became dissatisfied with the work and decided to move on. A discussion between Charley and me ensued. He wanted to return to New York state while I was for pushing West to Michigan, where D.H., after graduating from Ann Arbor was employed as civil engineer on the Northern Extension of the Jackson, Lansing, & Saginaw R.R. Unable to reach a decision even after arriving at the depot, we finally decided by standing a stick on end and going in whatever direction the stick fell. It fell West and we bought tickets of Jackson, Mich. From there we promptly went to Wenona [Winona] where we found D.H. Here we found that he was just on the point of changing to the Michigan Central, which was at that time building a line from Detroit to Lansing. His division was the first twenty-two miles out of Lansing. We went together to Ann Arbor where Charley decided to take a course in book-keeping and telegraphy. I returned to Lansing to begin my first railroading under D.H. as a rodman, laying out work for construction. We remained on this work for about a year altogether. During this time Charley having finished his course in telegraphy, secured a position as operator on the Michigan Central Ry."

63   Oxford, Michigan is located roughly 15 miles north of Pontiac, Michigan. Vassar is another 45 miles northwest from Oxford, with Otter

By May 21, 1873, the road was completed and trains running through. The railroad authorities wished me to remain on the line, but I preferred construction work and quit. Returned to Detroit on May 21. On this line just completed I lost $564.00 cash on account of a timber contractor, H.B. Blackman of Howell. He authorized me to make some timber contracts for him, then threw up on them, leaving me to make good the losses. This caused me no little embarrassment and mental suffering. I was without money and no work in sight. The financial crash of 1873 was beginning to be felt, in fact was upon the country and paralyzed public works.

How stood the ledger with me at this time, four years after graduation, and between 35 and 36 years of age? April 1, 1873, I sent Mr. E.B. Morgan a draft for $586.94 for the last two years at Ann Arbor. I had previously sent him about $700.00 for the first two and had paid that account in full. He wrote congratulations and compliments, and said he had not expected me to pay out anything like so soon.

I had paid Mr. Higley his bill about $75.00. Had bought and paid for a new transit $250.00, level, $100.00, and various other engineering necessities amounting to about $150.00, replenished my wardrobe and lost (by Blackman) $564.00 cash.

In the four years, then, I had earned and paid out for debts, instruments, and loss, $2375.00, besides board, lodging, clothes, and all other expenses. The railroads I worked for paid no bills, no personal account bills and furnished no instruments. And during this time I had

Lake lying between the two. Bay City, Michigan is 22 miles northwest from Oxford, at the mouth of the Saginaw River in Lake Huron's Saginaw Bay.

to learn to put into practice what I had learned of my profession. I started at $60.00 per month.

In May, 1873, Brother Will and I took the first three degrees in Masonry in Vassar Lodge #163.[64]

The remainder of May, '73, and the forepart of June I was at Detroit on expense and concluded to visit East. I borrowed of Brother Will $100.00 and on June 18, left for Aurora, N.Y. I received a most cordial welcome from Mr. Morgan, whom I had last seen in his library, nearly eight years since, and all other friends there, and though I was visiting on borrowed money, I think it was the happiest day of my life. The expressions of friendship, confidence, and esteem I received then and there from those whose esteem could not be easily earned was worth much to anyone.

They had all known me as a boy in the shop, store, Academy, and Army. I also visited at Auburn, Millport, Pine Valley, Watkins [Glen], Niagara. How many precious memories crowded my thoughts as I went about the old last home at the Valley. Strangers were living there now. "The garden walks by other feet were trod." And loved ones who had made it home were gone. It was a hallowed spot. Here I hastened when duty would permit as to a Mecca. Here I received embraces, tears, and Godspeed as I would be leaving, which burned into my very soul, an

---

64   As Rhodes later notes, this was the only fraternal organization he ever joined, apart from the Grand Army of the Republic. Rhodes remained similarly uninvolved in any political activities. Nowhere in his autobiographical account is any mention of a political leaning or preference, although we know from other sources that he was a Republican—not a surprising political affiliation for a non-drinking, Calvinist, veteran of the Union Army in an age when the Democrat Party was tarred as being the party of "rum, Romanism, and rebellion."

ever-present talisman for a better life. From here Mother and I went, when sick and weak she sought in change of air and surroundings rest and strength, not thinking as she kissed her little ones good-bye it was for the last time. Years had passed and if by study and labor I had learned to value life more and realized more the possibilities of it, I owed it to my good angel and indomitable perseverance. The task had been a severe one and I had to accomplish it alone, but thus far when I apply the test, "by their fruits," there is the rub, "the fruits"! Would to God I could point to something accomplished worthy of all this labor and all this struggle. But the spirit is still willing and the flesh is not weak.[65]

Returning, I reached Detroit August 2, 1873, $140.00 in debt. On the 23rd of that month I received a letter from George Paul, Chief Engineer of the Chicago and Atlantic R.R., saying to come to Kenton, Ohio, at once. I borrowed $20.00 of J.E. Howard and three days later (August 26th) was Division Engineer, Marion to Kenton, with my head-quarters at William Wiley's in Big Island. Construction was in progress. By fall the money failed and field work was practically suspended. Brother Will was my assistant. I was retained in the office until September 28, 1874, then quit. The company had not given me enough to pay my living expenses and owed me $1300.00. They were bankrupt and I never got a dollar of it. The panic was still on and such projects could not be floated.[66]

---

65   The biblical references are to Matthew 7:16 and to Matthew 26:41.

66   The financial crash of 1873 triggered a depression that lasted until 1879—the largest and most severe economic downturn in America prior to the Great Depression of the 1930s. Though triggered by a number of causes, including German economic policy and the tightening of currency caused by an American decision to move away from silver, speculative railroad investment

I remained in Kenton, Ohio, doing what local engineering work I could until January, 1875, when I made a plat and drainage survey for Scioto Marsh, near Kenton for John Gun, County Surveyor. I completed this work by April 5, '75. I did the work at his house on the farm. During that summer I made a grade and plat book for Kenton, William Strong, City Engineer.

In the fall of 1876 I went to Bellaire, Ohio, as Engineer on the Bellaire and Southwestern R.R. and was with that road until completed and trains were running to Armstrongs. Part of the time as Division Engineer and later as their only Engineer. This was a subscription road, with heavy rock cuts and many long high trestles. They paid for a time and then quit paying except a few dollars occasionally for board, etc. That is all I ever got. They would have paid but did not have the money. My office was at Mr. Hart's near Jacobsburg, from July 12, 1878, until winter set in.[67]

---

was both a cause and a victim of the crash. As he implicitly recognizes, Rhodes was at a fortunate point in his career when the crash hit—old enough to have paid off his education, young enough not to have incurred substantial additional debt, and still flexible and unattached enough to move to find employment, however unappealing, until new opportunities eventually opened up.

J.E. Howard (died 1912) was a railroad executive and associate of James F. Joy at the Michigan Central; he was later a member of the Michigan Railroad Commission and member of the board of trustees of Kalamazoo College. Kenton and Marion lie about 26 miles apart, in north central Ohio, roughly 45 miles north of Columbus; Big Island was a crossroads, five miles west of Marion. William Wiley was the postmaster in Big Island.

67   Bellaire, Ohio is in the mountainous eastern edge of the state, on the Ohio River just below Wheeling, West Virginia; Armstrongs Mill was a hamlet on Captine Creek, 12 miles as a crow flies or 22 miles by the shortest road; Jacobsburg is an unincorporated crossroads between the two.

I became disgusted and disheartened with such railroading financially. I was only paid enough to meet absolute expenses, only good will and promises for the rest. I was not accumulating anything. It was mostly the fault of the times. I got even with the world in '73, a most unfortunate time, yet I was fortunate in having paid my obligations before the crash came.

I determined to look to the West, and the first of May, 1879, wrote to A..A. Robinson, Topeka, Kansas, Chief Engineer, Atchison, Topeka, and Santa Fe Railroad to know if I could get work in the West. In a few days he wired me to report to W.B. Strong, Topeka, in ten days. Mr. Strong was then General Manager of the Santa Fe. At once I notified the Bellaire and Southwestern officers that I was going to leave and did. Mr. Mooney, the President, gave me $100.00 and on Sunday May 12, 1879, I reached Topeka and met my classmates there, Seely and Alexander. Seely was in charge of construction in Kansas. Alexander was attached to the Land Department of the road. Mr. Robinson was at Pueblo.[68]

---

68   A.A. Robinson, of course, was Rhodes's former University of Michigan roommate, now the strategic visionary and Svengali of the Santa Fe railway, building it into the largest railroad in America. William Barstow Strong (1837–1914) was a graduate of Bell's Business College in Chicago; Strong's father was a small-town merchant and temperance-hotel operator in Beloit, Wisconsin. Strong started his railway career as an assistant station master and telegraph operator, working his way up through various Midwestern railroads, including the Michigan Central, before joining the Santa Fe road in the late 1870s, serving as the president of the road from 1881 to 1889. Thomas J. Seely (died 1883) was another of Rhodes's classmates from the University of Michigan's Class of 1869. Seely had studied as a mining engineer, and was an assistant chief engineer for the Santa Fe road at the time of his death. As noted above, Alexander had roomed both with Robinson and with Rhodes at the University of Michigan. All of the men mentioned—Robinson, Strong, Seely, Alexander, and Rhodes—were rough contemporaries, about 40 years

They were all ready to commence construction from Wichita south to Arkansas City on the Indian Territory line. I was given a Division from Wichita south for twenty-five miles. On that same Sunday afternoon I left for Wichita and on Monday, May 13, 1879, I commenced work for the A.T.&SF RR at a salary of $125.00 per month with an allowance of $10.00 per month for use of instruments. I stopped at the Douglass Avenue Hotel, then the leading hotel in the city. I was now between 40 and 41 years of age with no assets but my surveying instruments and owed $150.00. It was again commencing at the bottom for the third time in my life—this time in the Great West, a terra incognita to me until the present.[69]

Wichita was the terminus of the southern branch of the A.T.&SF, a straggling, wide-awake, bustling frontier town. It was the shipping point for wheat for fifty miles beyond. A hundred wagons loaded with wheat waiting to unload was not unusual. Citizens, cowboys, frontiersmen, and Indians. A thriving frontier dance house with embellishments at the west end

---

old at this fortuitous time, as the country finally emerged from the depression of 1873 and another railway construction boom was beginning. Pueblo, Colorado, on the edge of the Rocky Mountains, was an important railroad hub and already at this time was developing a booming steel industry.

69   Note the speed with which Rhodes was able to move. In less than two weeks from when he first wrote to his classmate Robinson, he had quit his job, left his housing and wrapped up all personal affairs, traveled roughly 900 miles to a city he had never been (indeed, to a city roughly 400 miles west of any place he had ever been), met with his new employers, moved to yet another city yet another 140 miles away where he knew absolutely no one, found housing, and began work. In the next month, he would move two more times.

of the Arkansas River bridge made night a wild carnival of vice and crime.[70]

June 7th I moved headquarters to El Paso [ed: El Paso, Kansas, not to be confused with El Paso, Texas], boarded and roomed with a Mr. Minicke, in a brick dwelling at the east or north edge of town.[71] Mr. George B. Lake, at this time Superintendent at Nickerson, asked Mr. Seely to allow me to be transferred to his department (Operating Department). Seely consented and wrote me what Lake wanted. I was surprised, but I had been upon construction so long I thought I would like the change, so June 12, 1879, I went to Nickerson, Kansas, as Assistant Engineer, Operating Department, limits Nickerson to Pueblo and later to Las Vegas, New Mexico. I liked the work and the freedom it allowed. The latch string of Mr. Lake's home at Nickerson always hung out to me.[72]

---

70   With a population of roughly 5000 at the time, Wichita was probably Kansas's fifth largest city—— dwarfed by the metropolises of Leavenworth, Topeka, and Atchison, each of which had a population in the neighborhood of 15,000. Wichita's growth had been explosive, however. The census of 1870 showed it with a population of only 689. Arkansas City, with a population of about 1000 at the time, is located some 60 miles south of Wichita on the Arkansas River, about 5 miles north of the boundary of what is now Oklahoma and was then Indian Territory.

71   El Paso, Kansas is now Derby, Kansas. Is is about 12 miles south of Wichita.

72   Nickerson, Kansas is roughly 60 miles up the Arkansas River—that is northwest— from Wichita. Founded in 1872, it was named for the then-president of the Atchison, Topeka, and Santa Fe Railroad, Thomas Nickerson. From Nickerson, the Santa Fe's line ran 400 miles west across the Kansas and Colorado plains to Pueblo, Colorado, at the foot of the Rocky Mountains. Las Vegas, New Mexico was 200 miles south, along the front line of the Rockies. Pueblo and Las Vegas were key railheads for passage across the Rockies.

April 15, 1880, the following circular was issued:

> Mr. D.H. Rhodes, Assistant Engineer for Middle, Western, and Southern Divisions, headquarters at Nickerson, has charge of the repairs of bridges and buildings on those Divisions. Foremen of carpenters will make weekly reports to Mr. Rhodes, will make requisitions for material and supplies upon him, and call upon him for all needed instructions. They will be governed by Division Superintendents in matters not requiring the advice of a civil engineer.
>
> —George B. Lake, Superintendent

October 22, 1880, the following circular was issued:

> Mr. D.H. Rhodes, Assistant Engineer in the Department of Track, Bridges and Buildings, is hereby appointed Roadmaster, State Line to Pueblo, vice James Hireen, resigned. Mr. Rhodes will have charge of the Water Service on above Division and will also continue to act as Assistant Engineer on the Division from Nickerson to the State Line. His headquarters will be at LaJunta, Colo.
>
> —George B. Lake, Superintendent

This caused me to move to LaJunta, Colorado. There was nothing there. The depot was a double tool house. There was no laid-out town and no accommodations. It was frontier in fact.[73]

---

73   "The State Line" is a reference to the Kansas-Colorado state line. LaJunta, Colorado, on the Arkansas River, is roughly 65 miles east of Pueblo. It is a junction point where roads and railroads branch south toward Santa Fe.

Monday, November 8, I was thrown from a hand car into a bridge at Robinson. The car and four men passed over me. I was seriously injured but no broken bones. The evening train brought me back to Nickerson where I was under the care of my very warm and esteemed friend, Dr. F.M. Smolt.[74] I did not get out for several weeks and was under his treatment until December 16th.

May 20, 1881, the following circular was issued:

> The jurisdiction of Mr. D.H. Rhodes, Assistant Engineer and Roadmaster, has been extended and he now has charge of Track, Bridges and Buildings from Dodge City to State Line, headquarters at LaJunta. Mr. S. Harpster, Assistant Roadmaster, has immediate charge of track Dodge to State Line, headquarters at Dodge City. Mr. J.M. Woodward, Assistant Roadmaster, from State Line to Pueblo, office at LaJunta.
>
> —George B. Lake, Superintendent

By this time we had built a new depot at LaJunta, with offices upstairs and an old warehouse had been converted

---

74   Sic. Presumably Dr Charles F. Smolt (1854–1899), the Santa Fe doctor in Nickerson from 1878 to 1887, and again in the 1890s. Smolt had married into the Nickerson family. The site of the accident was presumably what is now the ghost town of Robinson, Colorado, 12 miles northeast of Leadville, Colorado, along the route of what would be the Colorado Midland Railroad. The almost impossibly difficult terrain of the upper Arkansas River valley as it penetrates the Rockies was fiercely and at times bloodily contested by the Santa Fe railroad and its rival, the Denver and Rio Grande railroad, and it was in the struggle to control these passes that Rhodes's classmate and now boss, A.A. Robinson, gained his greatest fame. As a crow flies the distance from Robinson to Nickerson is roughly 500 miles. For a seriously injured individual, this must have been a difficult and painful trip.

into a railroad eating house with sleeping rooms above and was run by Fred Harvey, who conducted all the railroad eating house hotels on the System.[75]

Friday, September 9, 1881, Mr. A.A. Robinson went east on a special. He has about completed the line to the Mexican boundary and removes his office to Topeka, and, as Chief Engineer, assumes jurisdiction of track, bridges and buildings over the whole line.

November 1, 1881. The following extracts are taken from a circular:

ORGANIZING THE RESIDENT ENGINEER SYSTEM IN THE OPERATING DEPARTMENT
CHIEF ENGINEER'S OFFICE, TOPEKA,
NOVEMBER 1, 1881

Mr. D.H. Rhodes, Resident Engineer, will have charge of T.B.&B. [track, bridges, and buildings] on Division No. 4, Main Line Ellinwood to State Line, office at Ellinwood, Kansas. J.M. Woodard will report to Mr. Rhodes, as Roadmaster in charge of track, Ellinwood to Cimarron, office at Ellinwood. Mr. S. Harpster will report to Mr. Rhodes as Roadmaster Cimarron to State Line. Mr. D. Hogbin will have charge of Bridges and Buildings,

---

75   Dodge City, Kansas was roughly halfway between "State Line" and Nickerson, Kansas. Rhodes was being given progressively larger duties and progressively larger stretches of railroad to look after.

Frederick Henry Harvey (1835–1901), in partnership with the Santa Fe road beginning in 1876, developed the concept of a restaurant chain, operated a string of restaurants and hotels along the rail line, and encouraged tourism. Roughly the same age as Robinson, Rhodes, and the other engineers and managers building the Santa Fe, Harvey came from an even more modest background than they —an emigrant, he started off as a restaurant busboy.

Ellinwood to State Line, office at Ellinwood, and will report to Mr. Rhodes.

—A.A. Robinson, Chief Engineer

November 4, 1881, opened my office at Ellinwood, building not completed, office in a box car for some time.[76]

We now began to realize the superior organizing capacity of Mr. Robinson. New life and great activity everywhere in his department. The Operating Department had developed no system, no uniformity, no standards and was without a head in the Track, Bridges, Building and Water Service. There was very little steel rail west of Nickerson, old iron rail but little better than scrap, clear through to Pueblo. Track was steel from LaJunta south. Ties so badly decayed that wrecks and derailments were of almost daily occurrence. It seemed that until now construction had been all absorbing.

Scarcely had Mr. Robinson organized his office when every mail brought us blueprint standards for every class of building, with specifications and bills of material—for signs, signals, and posts, for yard tracks, large and small, for roadbed, cross-sections for rock ballast and for earth surface, for cut ditching, in short, everything of this kind. Confusion and want of system at once disappeared. Order, symmetry, and neatness took its place under his superior judgment, skill, and organization.

I was in my element as never before, comprehended the whole scheme, was in perfect harmony with it, and never so

---

76   Ellinwood, Kansas is 30 miles west of Nickerson.

much enjoyed my work as then. It seemed to develop in me new life and capabilities not before called out. Authority and responsibility went together under him, and there was always sufficient of both. Steel rail began to come by train loads and ties the same and for a couple of years until the old iron and ties were all out, I had constantly ten to fifteen large extra gangs at work, and section forces largely increased. Scraper gangs were employed raising embankments for miles in the lower places. Iron trussed bridges upon masonry abutments replaced wood trusses on piles.

May 22, 1883, the following circular was issued:

OFFICE OF ASSISTANT GENERAL SUPERINTENDENT AND CHIEF ENGINEER, TOPEKA. WESTERN DIVISION

D.H. Rhodes will have charge as Resident Engineer of the Western Division. S. Harpster, Roadmaster, Dodge City to Blackwell. J.M. Woodard, Roadmaster Blackwell To Rockvale. E.C. Ward, General Foreman Bridges and Buildings, Dodge City to LaJunta. J.S. Kerr, do, LaJunta to Pueblo and Rockvale and from Division.

—A.A. Robinson, Asst. Genl. Supt. and Chief Engineer

In all approximately 500 miles.

These heads of departments all reported to and received their instructions from me. Division Superintendents had no authority over them.

This appointment took me back to LaJunta as headquarters again, and on June 1, 1883, I moved my office there. I had much the same class of work here as before putting in steel, ties, new yards. About this time the Division yard, roundhouse, and storehouse at LaJunta was built. Also the Coolidge yard, roundhouse, and Division buildings.

November 20, 1883, the following circular:

OFFICE GENERAL SUPERINTENDENT AND CHIEF ENGINEER, TOPEKA

W.W. Borst, Superintendent, Western Division, has resigned. D.H. Rhodes is appointed Superintendent, Western Division, headquarters at LaJunta, Colo. Effective November 25, 1883.

—A.A. Robinson, General Supt.
and Chief Engineer.

Approved.

—A.E. Touzalin, V.P. and Gen'l Mgr.

The Western Division covered 510 miles and lay in two states and one territory—Kansas, Colorado, and New Mexico.[77]

I got along nicely with my new responsibilities and enjoyed my work.

---

77   William Wallace Borst (1839–1915) was an outsider in Robinson's Santa Fe family, having been one of the lieutenants (literally— he had been one of the general's lieutenants in the Civil War) of General William Palmer, leader of the rival Kansas and Pacific, which had been acquired by Jay Gould's Union Pacific. The move to the Santa Fe was only temporary, and Borst rejoined Palmer.

Then the following circular:

GENERAL MANAGER'S OFFICE
TOPEKA, MAY 15, 1884

Mr. D.H. Rhodes having resigned the position of Superintendent of Western Division is this day appointed Engineer of the A.T.&S.F. R.R. to fill the vacancy caused by the death of Mr. George B. Lake.

—A.A. Robinson, General Manager

Approved.

—A.E. Touzalin, Vice President.

This appointment took me to the General Office at Topeka, and I had charge of engineering work over the whole line. Mr. Robinson still retained the title of Chief Engineer. My salary was now $300.00 per month. This was a fine position. I had fine offices and an excellent office corps. However, in time, I came to dislike it. The time was an interval between two periods of active construction work. Only the Magdalena Branch in New Mexico and the Wichita and Western into Kingman, Kansas, were constructed. Most of my work was on old matters and little original work. No record could be made. There was nothing to make it on. I felt I was not at my best, and sent in my resignation. It was returned promptly and emphatically— "Not accepted." I remained.[78]

---

78   At the risk of making too much of little evidence, it nonetheless seems typical that Rhodes's only comment on the death of one of his closest and longest professional acquaintances—the man whose latchkey was always out to him, and who had welcomed him with open arms and requested his reassignment only seven years before—is by quoting a telegram that

Then the following:

TOPEKA, KANSAS
MARCH 24, 1886

D.H. Rhodes is hereby appointed Chief Engineer of the Kingman, Pratt & Western Railroad Co. to locate and construct the extension of the Wichita and Western R.R. through Kingman, Pratt, and Kiowa Counties.

—Edward Knisely, President.

This was a joint A.T.&S.F. and St.L&S.F. [St. Louis and San Francisco] line to be located and constructed under separate management. My appointment came practically through Mr. A.A. Robinson.

This was more active work and suited me better although it took me out of the line of succession or off the main line, which I think was to my disadvantage in the end.

April 1, 1886, I opened an office at Kingman, organized a field corps of engineers, commenced letting grading and timber contracts, made bills and requisitions for everything required to build and equip eighty miles of road. Mr. Robinson countersigned my requisitions. The President lived in Boston. I was in full

---

indicates that because of this acquaintance's untimely death, Rhodes would now have his job. In discussing his adult life, nowhere does Rhodes make reference to friends outside the workplace.

Rhodes's drive to "make a record"—that is, to build something that would leave a mark—is made explicit here. If Rhodes's account of the 1884–1886 period is full and accurate, it would seem that Rhodes, in his pursuit of achievement and respect, felt that these needed to be found not in title or remuneration but in accomplishment.

charge and authority. I was myself again and my best found means of expression.[79]

July 13 we commenced track laying at Kingman. August 30 the first regular train ran to Cunningham and returned. After a long and stubborn legal fight we succeeded in getting the track through Saratoga, and November 30, 1886, the first regular train went into Pratt and returned. Reached Cullison in December and suspended construction until spring.

In the spring of 1887 we resumed construction. The first regular train into Greensburg was run on June 23. Construction was continued to the west line of Kiowa County.

August 8, 1887. Brother George died at Cairo and was buried at Kingman the following day.[80]

The following circular:

BOSTON, MASS.
JULY 8, 1887

Mr. Frank M. Hill, Superintendent of the Wichita and Western Railroad, is hereby appointed

---

79   Kingman, Kansas, 44 miles west of Wichita, was the terminus of the existing Wichita and Western railroad, a Santa Fe operation. The project was to extend this railroad through several more Kansas counties. Cunningham, Kansas was 18 miles west of Kingman; Pratt, 33 miles; the crossroads of Cullison, 44 miles; and Greensburg, 65 miles.

80   George Marcus Rhodes was the baby of the family. His death was from tuberculosis. He had gone to brothers Charley and Will to die; Rhodes appears to have taken care of the burial. Again, while it is dangerous to read too much into the narrative, the brevity of this interjection into the account of Rhodes's professional life is possibly indicative.

Superintendent of the Kingman, Pratt & Western Railroad. D.H. Rhodes, Chief Engineer of the K.P.&W is appointed Chief Engineer of the W&W also. Office at Kingman. Effective July 12, 1887.

—Edward Knisely, President.

Then the following:

BOSTON, MASS.
DECEMBER 27, 1888

Mr. Frank M. Hill having resigned, Mr. D.H. Rhodes is appointed Superintendent, Freight and Passenger Agent of the W&W and the K.P.&W. Railroads. Office at Wichita. Effective January 1, 1889.

—Edward Knisely, President.

On July 24, 1889, the two companies were consolidated into one, The Wichita and Western Railway Company.

In 1890 the line was turned over to the A.T.&S.F. to operate and I was without a situation. From May 15, 1884, to the present time my salary had been $300.00 per month.

In the winter of '85 and '86 I received a letter from Mrs. Lucy Coe of Newton, New Jersey, saying that her son, James, a young man was having trouble with his lungs and feared the climate of New York City was too severe for him and wished to know if there was not something he could get out west where winters were milder.[81] I had heard of nor from her in this thirteen years, did not know her husband was dead, or what family she had, or even if she was alive.

I wrote her I would do what I could for him. Soon as the K.P.&W. construction was assigned me, I wired for her son. April 15, 1886, he reached Kingman and I assigned him to the Engineering Corps, and he remained with the road as rodman and instrument man until the close of construction. He was a very intelligent and capable man. He being an only living child and the idol of his Mother, she, too, came to Kingman in the early fall of '86 and lived at Kingman. January 1, 1888, when I was made Superintendent and moved my office to Wichita, I took James Coe as Car Accountant and Store Keeper. His Mother then moved to and kept house at Wichita.

The renewal of our acquaintance after so long an interval was very pleasant and resulted in our being married at Wichita on November 26, 1889, by Reverend Mr. R.T. Savin, then pastor of the First Methodist Episcopal Church, Wichita.[82] We went to Chicago on our wedding

---

81   Mrs. Coe was obviously misinformed. In his notes for his manuscript, Rhodes included the following vignette: "January 7, 1887, was the coldest day and worst Kansas blizzard that I or any Kansan ever experienced. The railroad west of Dodge was lined with dead cattle that, drifting before the storm until stopped by the railroad fence there froze to death." This would have been James Coe's introduction to a Kansas winter. Fortunately he turned out to be a healthier specimen than his mother had intimated, and he adapted successfully to manhood in the Great Plains.

82   The First Methodist Episcopal Church, Wichita later became the First United Methodist Church. A brick structure at 320 North Broadway, Wichita, it was constructed in 1885 and demolished in 1949. Like that of many in boomtowns in the 1880s, the Reverend Savin's time in Wichita appears to have been very temporary: as late as 1885 he was a pastor at a mission church in Newark, NJ, and by 1891 he had relocated to Detroit.

trip and on our return we took up quarters in my rooms at the Carey Hotel and spent the winter there.[83]

My Brothers Charles and Will I had not seen for a number of years. They were in the mercantile business at LaRue, Ohio. They concluded to try the West. Will came ahead to spy out the land and reached Kingman June 3, 1886. He at once took charge of the construction material yard at Kingman. July 29, 1886, Will's family and Charles and his wife arrived at Kingman. Charles had been Station Agent and Operator and while getting a knowledge of the country, I made him Advance Station Agent to open and run them until the track reached the next one,

---

83   Wichita in 1888 was a boom town, quite unlike the place Rhodes had found in 1879 when he first joined the Santa Fe. In 1887, only New York City and Kansas City, Missouri had reported more real estate sales. And by 1889, Wichita had grown to 48,000 residents. See http://www. kansas.com/2011/01/29/1696734/keeping-up-with.html. The Carey Hotel (523 East Douglas Avenue, Wichita), now known as the Eaton Hotel, was built in 1886–1888 at a cost of $100,000, and is still standing. The hotel, which opened its doors in January 1888, was the cutting edge of modernity and is indicative of the extraordinary growth and sudden prosperity of Great Plains hub-cities like Wichita: it featured hydraulic elevators, steam heat, electric lighting, and a fire suppression system, as well as hot and cold running water in most rooms (though apparently bathrooms were still communal, at the end of the corridor). Ten years later, in December 1900, the hotel's bar, its huge mirror, and its painting "Cleopatra at the Bath" gained permanent fame as the target of a famous bit of vandalism by hatchet-wielding prohibitionist Carrie Nation. At the time Rhodes wrote his manuscript (1900–1911), the Carey Hotel would still have been among the best-known hotels in America. See: http://specialcollections.wichita.edu/collections/local_history/tihen/pdf/People&Places/Eaton_Hotel.PDF. These were good times, and Rhodes was riding high.

The crash for Wichita, as for Kansas as a whole, came in 1889, when droughts and the availability of land elsewhere led to the abandonment of newly opened farmlands, with predictable consequences for the rest of the overheated economy.

when he went forward again. Both he and Will gave excellent and intelligent service.[84]

In the summer of 1886 when the track had reached Saratoga, they purchased a stock of goods, built a store, and commenced business at Cairo, Pratt County, Kansas, Charles remaining as Station Agent.[85]

---

84   Because it offers an insight into the practicalities of Western migration, it is interesting to reproduce Will's account of how the decision was made and the facilitating role of family.

> "During the summer of '85 I took a trip to visit D.H. who was acting Chief Engineer of the Santa Fe Railroad at that time with headquarters at Topeka. He furnished me with transportation and I visited the following places: Colorado Springs, Manitou, & Las Vegas, N.M. I had a pass to Albuquerque but did not venture further West than Las Vegas. The purpose of my trip was to consider the possibilities of the new West, and upon my return I decided to cast my lot with Kansas. Charley acquiesced and we accordingly disposed of our interests in the store."

85   In 1910 Cairo, Kansas, a train stop between Kingman and Pratt, still had a population of 40. It has now (2013) completely vanished from the map, except for an auto repair shop. To give a flavor of the boom-and-bust nature of the opening of the Great Plains as the railways made agriculture potentially profitable, and of the direct role of the railways in this process, again brother Will's account is of interest.

> "The railroad company had laid out a townsite at Cairo, twenty-five miles west of Kingman in the Ninescah valley, and Charley and I located here and put up a store [in November 1886]. . . . Our store building was constructed by the time our families had arrived in Cairo. Our families occupied jointly the farm house which belonged to the townsite company. . . . The store building cost about $600. We put in a small general line. The country was sparsely settled but despite this fact the trade was good. Three years later on March 1st [presumably 1889, just as the Kansas bubble was about to burst] the store burned, a total loss of stock and building and no insurance. Immediately we began to plan for another structure. A two-story store building at Saratoga [nine miles away] was purchased, dismantled, and rebuilt at Cairo. In May the new store was re-opened for business. This time we put in a larger

As before stated the A.T.&S.F. commenced operating the W.&W. in the summer of 1890, and I was out of employment. Mrs. Rhodes and I took a trip to Colorado. Left home July 30. We had a most delightful trip, went up Pike's Peak and back by stage. September 30, Mrs. Rhodes started East to visit relatives in New Jersey. I went as far as Chicago with her.

Later the following:

TOPEKA, KANSAS
DECEMBER 10, 1890

D.H. Rhodes is hereby appointed Superintendent of the Panhandle Division, headquarters at Wellington, Kansas. Augusta to Englewood; Mulvane to Panhandle City, Texas; Attica to Medicine Lodge; Wellington to Hunnewell; Wellington to Caldwell.

---

stock of general merchandise. Fourteen months later during a severe thunderstorm the building was struck by lightning and burned to the ground. The fire took place late at night. We managed to save about $1000 worth of stock. The loss was about one-half covered by insurance. Continued droughts and the opening of old Oklahoma had almost emptied the country of discouraged settlers and we decided not to rebuild. … We lingered on in Cairo until November of the following year [1892]. Altogether we were in Cairo six years."

As had happened in the past, with the collapse of Cairo, Kansas, Rhodes rescued his brother Will, giving him a clerk's job with the Santa Fe. By 1895, brother Will was employed by the Santa Fe railroad in tearing up for scrap material stretches of Santa Fe track west of Cairo, Kansas that he and Rhodes had supervised laying.

In all, 550 miles. This was a new sub-division of the road.[86]

December 10, 1890, I moved to Wellington, organized the office force and commenced operations. My duties were laborious and exacting and kept me from home much of the time. Still my home life was charming. Mrs. Rhodes was not strong and vigorous, but she was a very intelligent woman, charming in her manner, pure in her ideals and her life, a devoted Christian wife. Home was a refuge and a joy.

August 14, 1894, Mrs. Rhodes and I left Wichita for a visit to Deckertown and other places in New Jersey. The 16th and 17th we spent at Niagara Falls, were gone about three weeks.

October 15, 1894, the Panhandle Division was by another subdivision of the road thrown into the Southern Division in part and part to the Southern Kansas Division. The Wellington office was closed. Two other Divisions were absorbed at the same time by lengthening the remaining Divisions. I was offered Trainmaster, the best at the time. I did not accept and was out of a situation.[87]

---

86   Wellington, Kansas is 35 miles south of Wichita. Panhandle, Texas, the terminus of the road, is 28 miles east of Amarillo. Panhandle was the link between the Santa Fe and a number of feeder railroads that brought Texas cattle to market, and the Panhandle Division was designed to be a major element of the Santa Fe's market plan.

87   Not mentioned by Rhodes is that in December 1893, the Santa Fe road had gone into bankruptcy, dragged down by larger market conditions across the Great Plains and Southwest. Equally significant, Rhodes's friend and protector, A.A. Robinson, left the Santa Fe at this time when he did not receive the presidency of the railroad, taking over the Mexican Central Railroad. The Santa Fe emerged from bankruptcy in 1896.

I commenced developing a patent track gauge I had had in mind for a year or more, but had not time to give to it. Perfected it and secured my patent letter. (May 23, 1896)

March 10, 1895, I was offered a position as General Foreman of Track, Bridges and Buildings on the Wichita and Western Ry. Now in charge of Receiver J.H. McIntire [i.e., in bankruptcy], since February 1, 1895. I accepted and commenced on the above date and moved to Wichita.

Up to this time I had had no home of my own. For more than thirty years had lived at boarding houses and hotels. I was now 57 years old, married and determined to have a home, make it comfortable and pleasant and with my good wife—please the Lord—spend there my remaining days. At once I bought a property (609 North Topeka Avenue), built, furnished, and moved into it.[88] Sunday May 26, 1895, we took our first meal in our new home. What a pleasure and what a joy to be living in our own home. We were both so proud of it, so contented that there would come times when it seemed like the peace and quiet that precedes disaster.

We had been there perhaps three months when Mrs. Rhodes, coming from down town had a very light stroke of paralysis in one side. It was more a numbness, affecting the circulation. After a few days it never interfered with her movements, hearing or speech to speak of, but she grew more and more nervous.

---

88   Presumably this is the two-bedroom, one-bath home still standing on the site, a two-story, frame building. The location is a half-dozen blocks north from the Carey Hotel, in what was then a fashionable neighborhood of Wichita. Brother Will, again out of work, supervised the construction.

April 9, 1896, I went with her to a Sanitarium at Quincy, Illinois. She remained there for a time, received little if any benefit from the treatment and came home. She slowly but surely grew more weak and nervous. Wednesday May [sic: June] 2, 1897, she went to Topeka to visit her son and family and to have medical care by Dr. Hogeboom.[89] The Sunday following (June 6) she was taken worse and we all thought best that she go to Stormmont Hospital, nearby, where she could have quiet and trained nursing. She went that afternoon. By Sunday, June 20th, she had become so weakened that she had to keep her bed for the first time during her sickness, except for a few days occasionally. At 1:20 A.M. June 25, 1897, she passed away.

We laid her weak and weary body to rest in the cemetery at Wichita, Kansas. She was born May 14, 1841, died June 25, 1897. Aged 56 years—1 month—11 days. We had been married 7 years—6 months—29 days. Always hopeful, helpful and true. A passionately fond mother, a devoted wife, a conscientious, active Christian.[90]

Then came the old, homeless life again, only more bitter and pathetic for the short sunshine and joy.

December 31, 1898 the Receivership terminated, and the Sante Fe Railway took over the road. I was

---

89   Presumably Dr. George W. Hogeboom (born 1831), former state senator and state representative and, until March 1897, the chief surgeon of the Santa Fe railroad.

90   Lucy Stoddard Coe Rhodes may well have been a passionately fond mother, but Rhodes seems to have been a less-engaged step-father. There is no further mention in his notes of Lucy's son, James Coe, and no suggestion in any records of any further interaction or communication between Rhodes and his step-son.

without employment. I had been in charge of the T.B.&B [tracks, bridges, and buildings] on the W.&.W. from March 10, 1895 to February 15, 1896 and from that date to December 31, 1898, Superintendent.

Early in the following year I received a letter from Mr. James Dun, Chief Engineer of the Atchison, Topeka and Santa Fe[91] and sent to Caney, Kansas, to construct a line from that point south about sixty miles into the Cherokee Nation. My title was Assistant Chief Engineer and the line had been privately projected as the Kansas, Oklahoma Central & Southwestern Railroad. (Something about the promoters, etc.)[92] I went to Caney and opened an office, organized a force, ordered material for track, bridges, buildings, and yards. Started the grading. Progress of tracklaying as follows:[93]

Laid first track at Caney, Kansas, May 19, 1899.
Track at Owen, I.T. [Indian Territory—i.e. what is now eastern Oklahoma], May 25, 1899 (R.L. Owen's Ranch)
Track at Lawton, June 20
Track at Dewey, July 4
Track at Bartlesville, July 15 (delayed by bridge over Caney R.)

---

91   This was the position that Rhodes had occupied under A.A. Robinson, and had left to build the extension of the Wichita and Western Railroad.

92   This appears to be a note by Rhodes to himself, indicating an intention to add material regarding the financial arrangements of this road. Note the hints that Rhodes offers later about graft practices associated with the construction of this road—something he had not mentioned in connection to other projects.

93   Caney, Kansas lies on what is now the Kansas–Oklahoma border, and was then the border between Kansas and sovereign Indian Territory, about 90 miles southeast of Wichita. The railroad ran directly south to Owasso, on the outskirts of Tulsa.

Track at Matoaka, August 24
Track at Ochelata, September 6
Track at Ramona, September 22
Track at Vera, October 4
Track at Collinsville, October 14
Track at Owasso, October 30
(Originally all the stations were named after Spanish American War commanders. We had to change this.)

As this line was through Indian Country we had much to do with them in the way of land and local material rights. General business was in the hands of white people entirely. (Squaw men) (Intermarried citizens)[94] Indians of no account for general business.

The coal properties at Collinsville were opened on arrival of trains. All "strip" coal, from five to seven feet stripping of earth. Bartlesville was the only existing town on the line at the time it was built, and we missed that village by about a half of a mile. Old Collinsville was a mile off the line, but moved over to the new townsite when the road built in. After the line was built, oil and gas were discovered in great quantities in Bartlesville and the region thereabout, especially two years later. An extensive traffic in oil developed for the new line. I could have bought lots and land in this region for a song. In fact I refused to accept outright gifts of property in Bartlesville. No thought of the buried wealth developed soon as the road was built. How many opportunities I have had for immensely profitable investments in my railroad

---

94   Again, these appear to be notes by Rhodes to himself, indicating topics on which he had intended to add material.

building, so often the pioneer, but did not realize the possible development. The pioneer is not the one to make money. The camp follower and speculator attends to that feature of frontier experience.[95]

The line was left dangling at Owasso on the banks of Bird Creek. The extension to Tulsa was not made until a few years later when the big oil discoveries around Tulsa made that town a most promising metropolis. I finished the construction of the K.O.C.&S.W. and left Caney, Kansas, for Wichita on February 27, 1900. Went to my fitted-up rooms in the Firebaugh Building.[96] Mr. Dun wrote me that there was nothing immediately in sight, and I settled down to await developments.

On April 14, 1900, I received a message from Mr. Norman Roff of Joplin, Missouri, to come to Joplin. Left next day. He is a brother-in-law of F.R. Gammon's formerly of the Santa Fe Land Department. Mr. Roff wanted me to be General Manager of the Consolidated Zinc and Lead Company of New York and Boston. (It was Mr. Gammon's idea.) My salary was to start at $250.00 per month and was to be increased to $500.00

---

95   Presumably these "gifts" were offered by the good citizens of Bartlesville to persuade Rhodes and others who might have influence to route the railroad through Bartlesville – or at least not further away. It would be far cheaper to offer Rhodes a piece of the town's prosperity than to have to relocate the entire town as the citizens of Collinsville had to do, or than to risk the even worse fate that a new town sponsored by the railroad would arise to take Bartlesville's place. Though this may be unfair, one reading of this passage is that Rhodes's regret seems to be that he did not have the foresight to guess that the land around Bartlesville was oil rich, not that the routing of a railroad encouraged speculation and graft.

96   A three-story brick building on North Market Street, near First Street, Wichita, built about 1890.

per month as soon as I made the stockholders some dividends. I accepted and took charge at once.[97]

The Company had three leases and two steam concentrating mills on each lease—a total of six mills. Also owned 350 acres of land. They had paid about $150,000.00 for the whole. I had accepted because it was a change for me and because I thought it would be pleasant.

The leases did not prove profitable, not much ore at either of them. For a time I was operating five mills.

On August 7, 1901, I was prostrated with typhoid. This original attack with two relapses, kept me from work until December 10th. It was the first run of fever I ever had. When through I felt fine and soon weighed more than ever before by twenty pounds.

I resigned from the Milling Co. on July 11, 1905. The going was too slow to suit me. During the time I took part interest in several small mines, that is, I "grub-staked" some miners who had some leases on supposedly mineralized land. But these ventures did not prove very profitable, but I continued to invest in various mining properties. There is an irresistible lure to prospecting.

January 1, 1906.[98] Have had no regular work since

---

97   Frank R. Gammon and Norman C. Raff were entrepreneurs best remembered for their brief role in the early film industry, as owners of the rights to Edison's "Kinetoscope." Gammon, Raff, and others capitalized Consolidated Zinc and Lead in 1899 in New York and Boston markets. Joplin, Missouri, situated close to the Oklahoma and Kansas borders, was the major economic center of southwestern Missouri at that time as well as the center of zinc and lead mining activity. At that time it was a metropolis of 26,000 people.

98   Although passages of the manuscript date from as late as 1911, most of the closing reflections that follow appear to have been written contemporaneously in January 1906, with the final paragraphs apparently

July last. Have been mining of personal account, but it has been mostly outgo so far. Always hoping, of course, to strike a body of paying ore. My outgo has been considerably more than my income for a year or more. So far I have sunk $5,000.00 in mines in this district with a return of 2% on the investment. The prospect at present is no more encouraging. I ought to stop, but hope to make up my losses as I do not like to admit failure.

Being no seer I cannot divine my horoscope or interpret the stars and signs at my birth to learn the leading characteristics of that direction we cannot see, but which seems to have some potency in the directing of the major affairs of our lives.

I think, however, from abundant experience my sign was an adverse one, for if I set my heart upon a thing or look forward with a particular interest to a personal event, I will meet with disappointment. If I anticipate more than ordinary pleasure at a prospective social event of any kind whatever, I am sure to be disappointed. If I plan a line of action, expecting more than usual results either in the way of investment, invention, or place, I am certain to be disappointed and fall short of anticipated results. More than likely signal failure. The more merit, the more signal the failure to realize what was anticipated. In short, anything I particularly count upon, if realized at all, is but partial and always disappointing.

This has become so prominent in the whole experience of my life so far that if I become especially interested in securing a situation in a prospective meeting, or an invention, in a prospective journey—anything, in fact, I know I shall

---

composed in 1909. In January 1906, Rhodes would have just celebrated his 67th birthday and entered his 68th year of life.

fail to realize my wish and aim. Desire will be the measure of disappointment. On the contrary, every success I have had, every desirable position, every unusually pleasant association or experience, every important turn in my life, every marked pecuniary advantage, has come unexpectedly from a source little anticipated. Strange isn't it? Yet, so strongly marked is this feature, so persistent, that I accept it as the rule, but not without trying to defeat it. While recognizing it, I have never acquiesced. Some marked illustrations:

When I came from the Army, I had about $200.00. Thought I would attend some school a few months and go back to commercial life. I went to Troy, Penna., to visit some relatives, returning I reached Elmira uncertain whether I should take the Erie Railroad to New Jersey, or go by way of Aurora, New York, where there was an Academy I knew of. It so happened (?) that the Canandagua and Elmira train came to the platform first. I took it. Should have taken the other, had it come first. This changed the whole course of my life. I spent two years at Cayuga Lake Academy in Aurora with no thought but one, and went from there to the University of Michigan and completed a four-year's course. I could not have anticipated this for I was $50.00 in debt at the Academy. I have been out of a situation a few times, applied in various directions, but the situation always came from a source I knew nothing of—in one case, a successful four year's engagement.

I married and built a home after I was fifty years old. I was interested in having a home at last and looked forward to home life so eagerly after my years of bachelorhood! In about seven years, wife dead, home broken up. But no need to multiply instances; there is scarcely an exception. Impromptu trips, social gatherings and such like events, as well as business matters prove pleasant and profitable only. I never seemed to be the architect of my own fortune. My life has been one of surprises. However promising, be it large or trifling, I must dismiss it from my mind as far as possible if I would not be disappointed. It is the unexpected that happens with me.

There is a direction in the affairs of life we cannot see. In all this I am not complaining, no particular occasion, only stating a well-observed fact.

I must have inherited a hatred of liquors. I would not take liquors, wines, or beers, even on a doctor's prescription, until after I was fifty. When I was a farmer boy twelve or fourteen, there was nearly always liquor in the harvest and hayfield. Boys of my age would drink from the square sarsaparilla bottle, but I could not be induced to drink. I hardly think it was principle then. I have been the lonesome one on many a fishing trip, picnic, and social gathering because I would not drink even a little. All my life I have shunned places where liquor was sold. Would not enter a saloon if I could possibly avoid it. No class of men do I hold in greater contempt than those who deal in it. I feel an indescribable pity for young men who drink, and loathe a drunkard.

I have always been fortunate in having friends who respected me and wished me well among both the high and lowly, for I have as much respect for a true man in lowliest employment as for the high in learning and authority. My confidence and respect seem to go out to the manhood of my acquaintances and not to the position they occupy. Never had many bosom companions. There ever seems an impassible barrier between myself and my associates. I do not desire it so, and have regretted it all my life, but do what I would, was never "hale fellow" with them. An impenetrable reserve seemed always present and seemed recognized by all. Neither myself nor others could break through. As a consequence I did not attach others to me so intimately or actively as others do. Though I had their respect and goodwill, not so often their warm active friendship. I did not seem to need it—though I missed it. Reading and study were always an acceptable substitute for company.

I could never sit about stores or loaf in market places any more than I could go without eating. To do so seemed to indicate an aimless life, lack of ambition, undignified. I never did it.

In religious matters I believed fully the fundamental doctrines of the Christian religion—the confession of faith, the Fatherhood of God, the divinity of Christ, and the gift of the Holy Spirit. Presbyterian in all but church membership. I prayed daily all my manhood life with faith and confidence. Was always averse to being governed by rules and by-laws. Joined but one society (Masonic) and seldom attended that. I think it was something of this aversion that held me back from joining the church, though my high ideal of what the outer as well as the inner life of a church member should be was some restraint. Felt I should be a communicant and expected to be some time. I felt myself to be a Christian but not a religionist. Did not believe any one church had a monopoly of Heavenly favors, but believed that to be saved one must live and act consistently up to the light one has. No doubt the consistent church communicant has a richer, fuller, spiritual life than an outside believer.[99]

It seems a misfortune that I have not enough of this world's goods to realize the comforts of a home and the physical poetry of living. Have had profitable employment, have earned a good deal of money, and should be a rich man instead of the possessor of a few thousand dollars. Have spent no money for intoxicants; never waged a game for even a cigar; never bet a cent on racing. My women acquaintances have been self-respecting ladies with whom it was a credit to associate and made only the ordinary demands upon my finances. All my business life I have had a surplus above expenses. Why have I not a competence at 68? Simply because I have not the shrewd business instinct that makes money by fair or unfair means. My investments have been in enterprises that failed or were unproductive. I felt that I could not take chances in large concerns and lost in the smaller ones.

In short, caution and literary tastes have prevented my being a success financially in the larger sense. People

---

99   Despite this comment, Rhodes appears to have been very sensitive to theological differences between denominations and to have taken them seriously. The final written entry in Rhodes's notebook, presumably from some time in 1920, is an excerpt from a letter to an old friend. In its entirety the passage recorded in his notebook reads:

"Such a time as I have keeping my Presbyterian plant alive with so many vigorous Methodist plants to crowd it. It is deep rooted however, and nurtured by loving memories and gives no sign of waning vigor. It seems that all who are and have been very near to me are, and have been, Methodists, except my mother, of blessed memory."

judging from my dress, associations, and habits of living credit me with having more money than I really have. That is at once pleasing and an embarrassment, as more is expected of me than I can afford sometimes. However, I generally contribute to worthy objects, believing it to be both the privilege and the duty of the good citizen.

Why have I not thus far married a second time? I have not had the heart to ask one I fondly respect to share in less than is really necessary to make a home for two. It does not seem wise at my age (70) to count upon increasing my holdings sufficient to realize the freedom from wasting care that one living as I have would consider necessary for comfort and happiness especially when one considers the increasing weaknesses that come with advancing years.

This seems cold and calculating when every fibre of my being rebels against the lone, selfish, wasting life I am living, and demands a home and loving companionship. How many times my heart has asked to sit in judgment in place of my head, but as the physical happiness of two would be at stake, I have not dared trust it to decide. I am not insensible how rapidly time is passing. "Justice counts less the things done than the intentions."

EPILOGUE

Rhodes married for a second time in 1912, at age 73, to Mrs. Mattie A. Youkey of Joplin, a widow. They lived modestly in Joplin.

In his retirement, Rhodes remained a significant and dominant presence in his family. In contrast with the days of his youth, however, when "family" included substantial numbers of Predmore and Rhodes uncles, aunts, and cousins of different degrees, "family" now was much more narrowly defined: brother Charley (until his death in 1911) and sister-in-law Anna who ran the Arcade Hotel in Ponca City, Oklahoma for eccentric oil baron Lew Wentz; brother Will (until his death a few month's before Rhodes's own) who operated a bank in Hennessey, Oklahoma, and sister-in-law Ida; and two nephews and one niece.

In retirement, Rhodes also assumed leadership roles with the Joplin post of the Grand Army of the Republic (the association of Civil War veterans, where he was "Colonel" Rhodes) and appears to have become a more active Mason. The preserved, written record indicates that Rhodes's reserved, Calvinist personality, restless physical and mental activity, crisp penmanship, and precise writing style remained unaltered with age. In addition to handwritten copies of important personal correspondence, Rhodes's notebook included lists of synonyms, word plays he found of interest, and passages he clearly meant to incorporate into letters or other writings. With more accuracy than the reporter probably knew, the *Joplin News Herald* noted in the closing paragraph of Rhodes's obituary: "He had unusual command of language and wrote prose and verse but never displayed it to anyone except intimate friends."[100]

Rhodes died—perhaps ironically of liver disease—in Joplin in August 1920, a few months shy of his 82nd birthday. Though his death was anticipated both by himself and by the family, in his surviving writings Rhodes himself made no reference to his impending passing or to any concerns he might have had about it. Twelve years earlier on the occasion of his 70th birthday, however, Rhodes wrestled with his thoughts on life and death, composing a poem that he shared with brothers Charley and Will and their wives:

> Seventy years to day, the records say,
> At Mother's side a new born infant lay;
> An heir to time, to death, to love and pain
> Then, back to the eternities again.
> A mystery pulsed in that infant breast,
> As pulsed in the cloud on Siam's crest.[101]
>
> Long the journey and devious the way
> Up to this year, this memorial day;
> From infancy, shrined in the Mother's soul,
> 'Till now, marking time at life's twilight goal
> By hastening childhood's lengthening year,
> When life was ecstasy or a tear;
> By youth, the portal of life's temple fair,

---

100   *Joplin News Herald*, August 29, 1920, p. 4.

101   Presumably a reference to morning – the sun breaking over the eastern horizon. Any literary reference is now obscure.

An Aeolian with discordant air;[102]
Past Manhood vigor, where a faith sublime,
Lured by the sweetest symphonies of time;
To age, where promise and fulfillment meet,
To glad the heart with worthy deeds complete,
Or tears, vain tears, and mockery of mien;
Or the wailing cry of Age, "It might have been."[103]

Through swollen veins the laggard currents flow,
Reluctantly the limbs respond, and slow,
Resting the long day in some friendly shade,
Watching the world grow dim, the faces fade;
Dimly the eyes reflect the sunset glow,
And how quickly their shallow founts o'erflow;
Voices so near, so clear, but yesterday,
Seem now so indistinct, so far away;
Pleasures seem a mockery of past delight,
When the world was young and the heart was light.

Where are the youths that joined me in the chase?
The maidens, coy, yet with such warming grace?
Mother, who taught my lisping tongue to pray?
Father, a silhouette through life's long day?
And one, whose "feet with Angel's wings would vie,"[104]
Where love or duty bid the wife comply?

---

102   That is, music in a natural minor key.

103   Presumably this is a reference to lines of John Greenleaf Whittier's 1856 *Maud Muller*: "For of all sad words of tongue or pen,/ The saddest are these: 'It might have been!'"

104   This appears to be a reference to the final lines of an anonymous 1810 poem, "A Fragment Found in a Skeleton Case": "These feet with angel's wings shall vie,/ And tread the palace of the sky!" This poem was widely republished in the nineteenth century, for example in journals that provided assistance to ministers in composing sermons, as well as in more general works such as *Christian Brothers' Advanced Reader, Specially Prepared to Elicit Thought and to Facilitate Literary Composition*, published by the De La Salle Institute in 1884.

I would wake me from these reveries, these dreams,
Slake my thirst of heart at the living streams,
Wake from this shadow land, this popied realm,
Yet, the fount of memory's Castalian stream.[105]

Then, when "Sunbeams drop their tints of gold,"[106]
When quick'ning strings the throbbing passions mold,
Make me a banquet, for each guest a bowl;
Not wealth and fame alone the feast may grace,
For love, for worth, for friendship make a place;
Let the Hall re echo like my boyhood hills,
A Nepenthe[107] for the wormwood life distils.

I hear no voice, no sound of gathering feet,
Not one invited guest appears, to greet;
The silence seems pulsing a sentient life,
Grasps the hand, folds me, soothes the mental strife;
Presses my tremulous lips, In the lull

---

105   The Castalian stream flowed from the sacred springs at Delphi, and
was employed by priestesses at and visitors to the oracular shrine. *Inter alia,*
one finds references to the Castalian stream in Sophocles's *Antigone,* Edward
Gibbons's *History of the Decline and Fall of the Roman Empire,* and John
Milton's "To My Father." In 1816 the essayist John Hamilton Reynolds
wrote playfully of writers and artists such as Samuel Taylor Coleridge,
Charles Lamb, and Leigh Hunt drinking from the Castalian stream.

106   This appears to be a reference to a passage from English journalist
and poet Edwin Arnold's *Light of Asia* (1879): "The sunbeams dropped/
Their gold, and passing in porch and niche,/ Softened to shadows,
silvery, pale, and dun/ As if the very Day paused and grew Eve."

107   Nepenthe was the classical Greek drug of forgetfulness. Rhodes presumably
would have been familiar with references to it in Edgar Allen Poe's "The Raven"
and in Percy Bysshe Shelley's "Prometheus Unbound." Earlier references
that he might also have been familiar with would have been in Homer's
Odyssey, John Milton's "Comus," and Alexander Pope's "Essay on Man." The
peculiarity of this particular passage, however, is that Nepenthe was thought
to have been distilled either from wormwood or opium, an assumption
Rhodes may well have been familiar with.

Of low, sweet melodies that seem to dull
The waking life-whispers, the feast is laid,
Come, feast, 'till the hunger of thy soul is stayed.

A gathering mist seems to cloud the Hall,
Voices dear, woo me from Memory's thrall.
I am but marking time at life's twilight,
Where two mysterious streams again unite
And ebb t'ward the echoless shore, for aye;
Boatman take thy fee, I give it willingly.

D.H.R. 1908

Dear Brothers and Sisters, though young in spirit and vigorous, still you may in perspective participate, to some extent, with me in the above sentiment.

Appendix

Among the notes that Rhodes left with his autobiographical account and that he appears to have intended to include was a chronological list he entitled "Some events that occurred about the time I was born in 1838." These provide an interesting insight into the variety of events and occurrences that Rhodes regarded significant. The list, in full:

1834	Lafayette died.
	Lucifer matches introduced.
	England emancipated slaves in the West Indies.
	McCormick invented the harvester and mowing machines.
1835	Colt revolver invented.
	Manufacture of pins.
	Chief Justice John Marshall died.
	Humboldt died.
1836	Seminole War in progress in Florida.
	Great Boer trek into Natal.
	Mexico's independence won from Spain. Santa Anna.
	Battle of the Alamo.
	Battle of San Jacinto, between Sam Houston and Santa Anna.
	Texas independence acknowledged.
	Wheatstone sent telegraph signals four miles.
	Louis Napoleon attempted to seize the throne of France, failed and came to America.
	After much experimentation, Pennsylvania was beginning to use the new fuel, coal.
	James Smithson gave $515,169.00 to found the Smithsonian Institution. Foundation laid.
	James Madison died. 85 years old. When he was first elected President, there were no railroads in the U.S. Now there are 3,000 miles constructed.

1837	Queen Victoria succeeds to the British throne.
1838	Chicago incorporated. Population, 4170.
1839	Daguerre invented sun prints (the daguerreotype). Locomotive "North Star" made 37 miles an hour. First power loom for making carpets. Goodyear got a patent for vulcanizing rubber.
1840	Morse got first American patent on telegraph. Napoleon's remains brought from St. Helena.
1841	Adhesive postage stamps first used. Poe, Longfellow, Cooper, Emerson were writing.
1842	First submarine telegraph lain from Governor's Island to New York City. Kit Carson found the Southwest Pass through the Rockies.
1843	Dedication of the Bunker Hill Monument with Daniel Webster, the orator. Foundation stone laid by Lafayette.
1844	Morse constructed the first telegraph line, Baltimore to Washington.
1845	Poe's "Raven" printed.
1846	Howe secured a patent on his sewing machine.
1847	Came the rotary printing press.

www.ingramcontent.com/pod-product-compliance
Lightning Source LLC
Chambersburg PA
CBHW070931210326
41520CB00021B/6897